TIME TO SAY HELLO

Katherine Jenkins is an international singing superstar who has redefined a music genre: she has brought classical music to the masses and inspired young and old with her incredible voice, her glamorous looks and, above all, her love for music, her country and her fans.

Born in Neath, South Wales, Katherine won national acclaim as the BBC Welsh Choirgirl of the Year and soon after a place at the Royal Academy of Music. And so began Katherine's meteoric rise to stardom.

Time to Say Hello is Katherine's incredible story. Packed with laughter, adventure, heartbreak and music, it is the tale of a dream coming true and one that will keep you gripped to the last note...

TIME TO SAY HELLO

Katherine Jenkins

LARGE
PRINT

First published 2008
by Orion
This Large Print edition published 2008
by BBC Audiobooks Ltd
by arrangement with
Orion Books

Hardcover   ISBN: 978 1 408 41321 0
Softcover   ISBN: 978 1 408 41322 7

British Library Cataloguing in Publication Data available

Printed and bound in Great Britain by
CPI Antony Rowe, Chippenham, Wiltshire

*In loving memory of my dad Selwyn,
my nanna Barbara Evans and Ieuan Thomas.*

For Mum and Laura

CONTENTS

PROLOGUE

I have only ever been scared, really scared—and feared for my life—twice, and neither of these occasions had anything to do with stage fright, or standing on stage in front of a huge audience or having lunch with the Queen.

'Missile alert at rear! Missile alert at rear!' are not words I ever expected to hear when I became a singer, but when I heard them called out one day as I was travelling between bases on my first twelve-hour whistle-stop tour to entertain the troops in Basra and nearby areas in Iraq, it was for real. I was terrified—even more so, perhaps, because I had been having a doze and was at my most relaxed when this happened.

As I experienced the G-force of the helicopter falling (later I was told it had plunged 1,500 feet in seconds, dropping from 2,000 to 500 feet), I glanced at the soldiers opposite me, who looked every bit as petrified as I was. Not surprisingly, I started screaming.

While the helicopter was still plunging down, the pilot had to tilt its nose so that he could try to see where the missile was coming from and, as a result, we were rocking and rolling about all over the place. 'Oh, God!' I thought. 'This is it. I am going to die.' Then, because the backs of the Merlins are open and you can see out, I saw anti-missile flares going out from each side of our helicopter.

There is absolutely no doubt that if the ground-to-air missile aimed at us had hit its target, my life and that of everybody else on board would have been brought to a sudden end. But, thanks to the Merlin's supersensitive early warning system, and the pilot's brilliant manoeuvring and evasive action, which included the firing of the decoy flares while we were still plunging a couple of thousand feet, we eventually landed shaken—and most certainly stirred—but unharmed in Shaibah, the largest British base in Iraq. And I was able to begin my work as the new Forces' Sweetheart.

*   *   *

The other occasion when I was scared out of my wits, and could so easily have lost my life, was when I was returning to my flat after an evening out in London celebrating a friend's birthday . . .

But before I write about this, let me tell you about its beginning. As my family and friends are so fond of telling me, I have a habit of jumping the gun, and I really should start this book, my life story, from the beginning. After all, before I reached my early twenties and came to London to study at the Royal Academy of Music, life had never been dull. Far from it. From the age of four onwards, one excitement followed another.

So, with that in mind, I will keep those stories for later chapters, by which time I will have reached the point when I was a student at the Royal Academy of Music and, later, en route to entertain the troops in Afghanistan. That will leave me free right now to back-track to those early *fablous* years. (*Fab-lous*, by the way, is my all-time favourite word, which I pronounce Welsh-lilt style, as two words, exactly as it is written here. I will try not to use it in every other sentence of this book, but I can't promise. Just think of it as my catchphrase!)

ONE

BLESSINGS

The first time a journalist said to me, 'You must have been sprinkled with stardust the day you were born,' I was reduced to giggles. I'd never heard that silly expression before, and giggling is what I always do when I feel shy, uncertain or overwhelmed. After she'd left, however, I thought, if that was her way of saying I was blessed, I couldn't agree more. I have been blessed in so many ways: blessed to have been born in Wales; blessed to have had Mum, Dad, Nanna and my lovely sister, Laura, in my life; blessed to have such good aunties, uncles, cousins and girlfriends (Kristy, Katie, Jane, Sophie, Kelly, Mary Rose, Gemma and Polly); blessed to have had such good friends and teachers; and blessed to have been given a voice that has enabled me to realise so many dreams.

My mum, Susan, met my dad, Selwyn, who had been married once before, when he lived in the same street as she did, eleven doors down to be exact, in the house where I spent my childhood and teenage years. That house, where we had so many blissfully happy times, was in Wellfield Avenue, a lovely street. A three-bedroomed, semi-detached council house, which my parents eventually bought under the government's 'Right to Buy' scheme, it had a front garden, five steps up to the front door, a small lounge, an extension at the back for the bathroom, three bedrooms upstairs and a long back garden. As both my parents were keen gardeners, they had a greenhouse where they grew cherry tomatoes (the best I've ever tasted) and cucumbers, and outside a whole wall of fragrant sweetpeas.

After Dad met my mum, they dated for about seven years before getting married, and soon after this, discovered I was on the way. I get the impression from Mum that I wasn't planned but that I was 'wanted'. That, then, was the first of my many blessings when I was born on 29 June 1980.

Throughout my childhood, my mum, who's a bit smaller than me at 5ft 4in, with short blonde hair, lovely blue eyes and the same big, wide smile as me, worked as a radiographer at a local NHS hospital, which was just a five-minute drive from our house. I remember once that Laura asked Mum whether a radiographer was a person who mended radios. We soon realised though, that Mum's job was slightly more important than that.

Both Mum and I are very open people who like to externalise things by talking about our problems, and airing whatever's on our mind with friends and loved ones. Likewise, just like me, Mum is very sensitive, doesn't like to get into an argument and will do anything she can to avoid them. I must say, born as I was in June, I am a typical Cancerian who will walk sideways (just like the crab that is the symbol for that star sign) to avoid anything disagreeable such as confrontations or rows.

Mum, who became our family's main breadwinner after my dad took early retirement, has always been a great inspiration to me. A very hard-working lady, with an exceptionally strong work ethic, she has always been an excellent role model who inspired both me and Laura to be honourable and independent, able to go out into the world and make money to support ourselves—and to always leave our plates clean! I have a great appetite and Mum's cooking is the best!

Dad was twenty-three years older than Mum, but that's not something you notice as a young child. I became aware of the difference in their ages only when I was in my early teens, the age when it doesn't take much for children to find something embarrassing about their parents. The first occasion I remember being embarrassed by having a father who was older than most of my friends' fathers was when I was with Dad queuing up for ice creams. 'There you are, darlin',' the ice-cream man said. 'This one's for you and this one's for your granddad.' And that wasn't the only time that kind of thing happened.

As I grew older, though, I realised what an amazing father my dad was, and I honestly believe that I am as grounded as I am today only because he was an older dad. He was so settled in himself, so calm, so worldly-wise, sensible and mature. He was brilliant at giving sound advice, and now I've learned that not every father and daughter get on as well as we did, I often think how lucky I was.

A slim, slightly built man, my dad wasn't very tall (around 5ft 8in) and had beautiful silver-grey wavy hair that defied any attempt to tame it—not that he ever wanted to. He used to joke that he slept on a corrugated pillow! He always wore glasses. For me, the very best thing about him was his sense of humour. He was so funny, a natural-born comedian, who could reduce us all to hysterics. In fact, the first thing most people say about him was how much fun he was to be around. For example, whenever we were in a party situation with the family, or out in the car, he would always crack jokes or get up to silly antics that made everybody laugh.

One occasion I particularly remember was a New Year's Eve when we had been to a party at my Auntie Jo's—my mum's sister. When he left the party, Dad had taken my cousin's toy megaphone and made announcements to every street they passed through that 'The water will be turned off at 6 a.m.'—and then insisted on singing through it all the way back to our house. He did, fortunately, have a lovely singing voice and could croon, as people were fond of saying, just like Matt Munro, whom he loved. But I don't think many people were very impressed that night when he danced down our street doing his impression of Gene Kelly's 'Singing in the Rain'. Even now, neighbours remember that night and often comment on it when they see me.

Although he loved entertaining others, my dad was, in fact, a very private person; and because he died when I was still so young—just fifteen years old—there's a lot I don't know about him. Sadly, too, because he was so much older than Mum, we are not incredibly close to his side of the family. He was one of five children: two boys, including himself, and three girls.

What I do know, because he told me, was that his great ambition was to be a pilot. He took all the exams and passed, but right at the end he failed the medical because he was colour-blind. The only colour he could see was yellow. Laura and I always made the most of this when we were children. We were forever larking around and saying, 'Dad, what's your favourite colour?' just to hear him say

4

'yellow' yet again. 'What colour are daffodils?' we'd ask as we collapsed with laughter. We also coloured all his birthday, Christmas and Father's Day cards yellow.

When his first ambition was thwarted, he decided to go into the Navy, joining the Fleet Air Arm, and was lucky enough to be based in Australia, which he came to love. He was billeted with a Welsh family who'd been out there for many years. Later, when he came back to Neath, he got a job as the man responsible for distribution with the Metalbox Company, the best-known factory in our town, which made tin boxes and cans.

I was almost two years old when my sister, Laura Ellen, was born under the star sign of Gemini on 10 June 1982, and I so wish I could remember peering into her cot and seeing her for the very first time. But I can't. In fact, I don't remember much about being two years old. I know some first-borns experience jealousy when a second child arrives on the scene, but I don't think I did. I just remember her as my little friend, who was always there. My most vivid early memory is sitting on our lounge carpet, basking in self-importance, as Mum taught me to write my name with crayons in a little book. I recall that moment, as I sat copying what she was doing, with such love. I had Mum's undivided attention—something no child ever gets enough of—and I was relishing the fact that she was teaching me something really important.

My second early memory is being taken to my nursery school, seated on the back of Mum's bike. It was summer and I just loved the sensation of the breeze ruffling my hair and tickling my face. I thought sitting on the back where everybody could see me was so 'cool'—far preferable to being hidden away inside the car.

Laura and I weren't exactly inseparable when we were growing up, but we were always incredibly close. As we lived in a small, tight-knit community, we shared the same friends and, when not playing with them, I remember inventing clubs of which Laura and I were the only members.

We were certainly not couch potatoes. Mum and Dad always encouraged us to be active, kept us busy around the house or took us out on adventures. Our energy—and there was plenty of that around—was always channelled into something creative, even if it was just 'Okay girls, go and play with the dressing-up box.' One of our favourite pastimes, in fact, was going over to Auntie Betty's and dressing up in her old clothes and high-heeled shoes. We'd put make-up on each other, do each other's hair, then, having made our entrance in front of everyone, we'd sing a song. We particularly loved to sing hymns or songs from musicals, such as *Les Misérables*, at our family parties.

Laura sings very well. She could easily have had a career in singing herself but (thank goodness!) she never had the passion for it like me, or the same pressing need to perform. She is, though, a very talented pianist—much better than I am when it comes to tinkling the ivories.

I've always thought we look very much alike, but others remain divided on this subject: they either think we look like identical twins or not at all alike—nothing in between.

Like our dad, Laura is very funny—she has a very dry sense of humour. She is also very clever.

She excelled in all her school exams, got a great degree and backpacked around the world before setting off to work in London for a company called Shared Intelligence. We are always joking that she must be a spy; her degree would certainly qualify her for that, and we know that when preparing to come to London she applied for a job at MI5. We'll never know for sure. Whenever I ask her about what she actually does, she says, 'Oh, I'm working for the government.' 'What does that actually mean?' I press, but I only ever get the vaguest of answers. That means she has to be a spy, doesn't it? I guess she can't tell me because then she'd have to kill me!

Laura's a very easy-going, serene person and everyone who meets her loves her because she's such good fun to be around. Mum and I are quite outgoing and Laura is, too, but she is a softer, more private person than either of us. That's always made me feel very protective towards her, especially after we lost our dad to cancer when Laura was only thirteen.

When I read what she had written about me in a 'Relative Values' feature, published in *The Sunday Times*, I cried. She mentioned things to that journalist that she had never mentioned to me— things like how she really didn't like it when other people touched me and how, at such moments, she always thought, 'She's my sister. I don't want other people touching her.' I was so moved by that because, although I've always known that she loves me, she had never expressed her love in quite that way and it made me realise just how much she cares and how protective she is of me. I also found it very touching to read how she felt about my singing: 'I knew Katherine had a special voice from very early on,' she said, 'and we knew she'd do something big.'

She spoke in some depth as well about other things we had never discussed, like me being attacked that night in London. Even though we are close, I had no idea she was quite so protective about me and that article was a real eye-opener. I guess our closeness stems from our mum, who was one of four children—she had an older brother, a twin sister and another sister who is six years younger. She has always been very close to her sisters, regarding them as her best friends in fact, and Laura and I grew up with the same feeling.

*   *   *

The other most important person in my life when I was growing up—and the only grandparent I ever had—was my mum's mum, Barbara Evans, whom we called Nanna. A really lovely lady, she was the unchallenged head of our family, for whom we all had the greatest respect. If there was ever anything that needed to be said or done, it was Nanna who said it or did it. Having been born in Scotland, she eventually moved to Manchester where, during the Second World War, she met and married my grandfather, who was from Neath. A glamorous lady, who always wore make-up, a bit of jewellery and a fabulous hat and coat for church, she was a hairdresser before she became a mother. I am sure it is down to her that I've always loved doing my own and other people's hair. Curiously, though, Nanna never did our hair.

As I mentioned earlier, my dad was brought up

in Wellfield Avenue, which happened to be the street where Nanna lived, just eleven doors away from our house. Likewise, all my aunties—her other daughters—and their children, my cousins, lived just a stone's throw away.

Neath, nestled as it is in a gorgeous green valley with a river running through it, is a lovely old market town in which to live, and there is much history attached to it and its immediate surroundings. Neath has always been renowned for being a close-knit community and, however far its residents may travel to fulfil their various destinies, friends remain friends for life.

Now that Laura and I both live in London, we'd love Mum to come and join us here, but we know she never will. Occasional visits are fine, but it would be far too much of a wrench for her to leave Wales, and we just have to accept that. Also, if the truth be known, wherever I travel and put down roots in the future, Neath will always be my true home. I don't think Laura or I could bear to break the cord that binds us to there. I still try to go home at least once a month to spend the night with Mum, and I would miss it so much if I didn't have a home there.

Looking back, I wouldn't change a single thing about my childhood. It could not have been a happier time.

TWO

'GOING DOWN THE GARDEN TO EAT WORMS'

Earthworms may not figure very large in most people's consciousness, or score many points when it comes to charisma, but they hold a very special place in my life. Just four years old, I came running out of primary school, past the Lollipop Lady, to where my mum was waiting. Bubbling over, I squealed, 'Mum-Mum, we're going to have a show at school—a talent show—but I don't know any songs.'

'I'll teach you a song,' Mum said. And, of all the songs she could have picked, she chose 'Going down the garden to eat worms', a song that is accompanied by a load of hilarious hand actions, and a song that I have never been able to live down since. Indeed, my most recent rendering of this masterpiece was on *Parkinson* in 2006, while sitting alongside Parky and between his two other guests, Dame Judi Dench and Lenny Henry.

Nobody likes me, everybody hates me,
going down the garden to eat worms.
Big ones, small ones, fat ones, thin ones,
see how they wiggle and squirm.
You just bite off the heads and suck up the juice
and throw the skins away.
Nobody knows how I can thrive on worms three
times a day.

Not surprisingly, Lenny rolled his eyes around and couldn't keep a straight face throughout, especially when I got to the line

Big ones, small ones, fat ones, thin ones,
see how they wiggle and squirm.

'What are you looking at?' Parky asked Lenny, as I reached the end of the ditty.

'I'm trying,' replied Lenny, who is renowned for seeing double entendres in everything, '*not* to look at anything.'

Anyway, having taught me this song at the age of four, Mum put me in a cute little patterned dress with a white collar and white tights, and tied my hair into bunches. When I came on stage, the outfit made an impact on all the mums, dads, uncles and aunties, with calls of 'How cute', and laughs of appreciation echoed around the hall. Ieuan Thomas, the headmaster, who has remained a great family friend of ours, was introducing the various acts that night. Placing his hands on my shoulders, trying to restrain me, he began: 'Ladies and Gentlemen, this is Katherine Jenkins and she's from the Reception Class . . .'

From my point of view, an eager-beaver novice artiste who was just bursting to get started, he seemed to be going on forever and, as I couldn't wait to sing, I kept interrupting him, trying to begin my song. 'Hang on a minute,' he kept saying, by which time the audience was reduced to hysterics.

By the time he surrendered and left me alone on the stage I was beside myself with excitement and, without wasting another second, launched into my Worm song. Then, as the last note trilled its way through the hall, the audience, only too aware that I'd put my heart and soul into the number, erupted into applause. After that momentous event, everybody who came to our house was subjected to a rendering of the Worm song—and, dare I say it, they still are! (My mum has it on tape!)

I honestly blame my mum. If she'd taught me a different song, my very first stage performance might have ended differently, and my life might not have turned out the way it has. As it was, I was smitten, my future career decided there and then in that little church hall next door to Alderman Davies, my Church of Wales primary school. All I ever wanted to do after that first sweet taste of success was to sing and my ever-obliging mum set about teaching me my second song, 'I'm a Little Teapot', also accompanied by hand actions.

The other person I have to thank for my early repertoire is definitely the above-mentioned Ieuan Thomas. He was, and still is, such a lovely, inspirational man—never a distant scary headmaster. A born teacher, who really had a vocation for the job, he always made a point of letting us get to know him by taking group singing classes himself all through our days in primary school.

We loved his sessions. We'd sit cross-legged on the floor around the piano in the assembly hall and he'd teach us songs so we could have a good sing-song together. I would sit as close as I could possibly get to the piano, throw back my head and sing my heart out. In no time at all, we would work our way through the song book, singing 'Bananas in Pyjamas', a really funny song that begins 'Bananas in pyjamas are coming down the stairs', followed by

'Hungry, hungry, I am hungry, table, table, here I come . . .' These were moments I would never forget, and now that Ieuan and I are friends, I am always teasing him, saying that on my next album, I am going to include hidden bonus tracks of 'Going down the garden to eat worms' and 'Bananas in pyjamas'.

I never lacked opportunities to perform. Between the various end-of-term events at school, we used to have lots of family parties, where my renderings of these songs were always top of the running order. I also loved going to visit my cousin Beverley, who has Down's syndrome and lived in a care home. Once there, I would put on a show and all the songs would come out again.

Since those days, people have often asked me: 'When did you realise you had a good voice?' but I don't think it ever dawned on me. I just wanted to sing. I didn't think about how I sounded, just knew that I was never happier, never more fulfilled than when I was singing to myself or others, and putting on shows, especially when Laura joined in.

*   *   *

Dad continued to work at the Metalbox Company until I was six. Then he took early retirement and became our house-dad when Mum decided to go back to work in the radiography department. We were lucky. He was a great cook and his whole life revolved around us. Mum always says that one of her favourite memories of him was when either Laura or I would climb on to his knee and he would sit there chatting to us. He was such a kind, conscientious dad. Although we could easily have walked home from school, he picked us up every day, then ferried us to our piano and singing lessons and choir practices.

Looking back now, I really appreciate all he did in those days. We were two very high-spirited little girls, very good at winding Dad around our little fingers and getting our own way, and quite a handful, but he never nagged or gave vent to anger. He always made it clear, however, if we had done something wrong and he was cross with us. His way of dealing with this was to give us the silent treatment, a very effective way to make a point and bring us to heel. Much later, when we were at comprehensive school, he found another equally effective way of punishing us—one that we dreaded.

Laura and I, and indeed Dad himself, absolutely loved the TV series, *Neighbours*, and Dad used to tape this every day at lunchtime so that when we got home from school at about three-thirty, we could all snuggle down, watch it together and not have to wait until the early evening. From then on, if we ever misbehaved, it was a case of 'Okay. You're not seeing *Neighbours*.' That did the trick. To miss an episode was sheer torture, but never quite as awful as knowing we had upset Dad. He really was everything to us—and we were to him.

*　　　*　　　*

Another very special moment in my early life was when I joined the choir at the local church, where Mum was a Sunday-school teacher. I was just seven years old and this was my first introduction to classical and religious music which, from day one,

14

became a passion. A little later, when I said I wanted to go away on summer choral courses, Mum would say, 'Are you sure? Is this really what you want? It'll be the summer holidays and you won't know anybody there.' She'd then talk me through it, but when she realised I was sure, that was it. She never tried to dissuade me, but neither she nor Dad ever pushed me into anything.

The truth is I never needed any prompting to do these activities. Even as a child, I was always driven, always on the go, never happier than when I was busy. One of my most vivid memories is being in Nanna's house and saying in a very anxious, intense voice, 'Nanna, I want piano lessons.' I was only seven, had only recently joined the choir, but I was convinced I would miss the boat if I didn't start piano lessons at once. Somehow, I'd got a bee in my bonnet that if I was going to be a good singer, I needed to be able to play the piano—and possibly every other instrument under the sun. Mum and Dad didn't have much money left over for such extras, but somehow they always managed to scrape enough together for things like that. Dad never grumbled, and was always ready to ferry me around like a taxi-driver. He really was a great support, and always made me believe that if I worked hard at it, I could achieve whatever I wanted. And work hard, I did.

Laura also joined the choir when she was six and continued until she was seventeen. Although there was a lot to do—choir practice on Thursdays, two services on Sunday morning, including Eucharist and Evensong—it was also a social thing. We attended a choir club on Fridays, run by a lovely man called Mr Norton, who took us out for regular

15

treats, such as the cinema, bowling or ice-skating in Cardiff. This was great because there were about sixteen of us child members at any one time, including many of our friends. Although most of the children loved singing, the choir club was a very clever idea that kept everybody going for a very long time—not an easy feat for many church choirs.

While we were members, Laura and I often put on concerts with the other children to raise money for the church. Laura, who was always too shy to sing solo, would do a piano recital and I would sing. Like me, she loved music, but our approach was always very different. From a very early age, she disliked being the centre of attention and hated performing, whereas I was always in my element when given those opportunities. Likewise, Laura loved learning and playing the piano, but what she loved best of all was playing for herself. She hated the exams. The examiners were really quite stern and poor Laura would be shaking like a leaf as she tried to do her best under such difficult circumstances. I learned the piano, too, but singing always remained my first love.

*   *   *

When I was ten years old, an incredibly exciting thing happened in our family. One evening when Dad was checking his football coupon, he discovered he had won £500—a huge amount of money for us. When he double-checked and the result was still the same, the house positively throbbed with excitement. After a few celebratory jigs around the house, followed by some serious

16

discussion, my parents decided to use the money to turn our third bedroom into a bathroom, complete with a shower, something we'd never had before. It was a truly lucky win that has remained etched on our memories—and I'm so thrilled my dad had that excitement.

When I think back to our childhood, I appreciate just how good Mum and Dad were at keeping us entertained. Televisions might have become a fixture in most people's homes by then, but we were never parked in front of one for hours on end. Both Mum and Dad always found the time to take us to the park or keep us active in other ways. For as far back as I can remember, I always daydreamed about being on the stage with home-grown Cardiff-born superstars such as Shirley Bassey performing 'Diamonds Are Forever' or Tom Jones doing 'Green, Green Grass Of Home' or 'It's Not Unusual'—songs that were forever being played on the radio when I was young. 'Wouldn't that be something, to sing with Shirley or Tom,' I used to think. I had no idea then that such things would come true for me.

*   *   *

Although I was always ambitious and driven where singing was concerned, I was also fairly easy-going, always up for fun, especially if it involved anything artistic like dancing. Always a girlie girl, interested in everything pink, I had the entire Barbie doll collection (never brand new—I think we probably found them in the church jumble sale!), including all the Barbie accessories, such as the house, the hair salon, the TV studio, and the pony stable. All I

17

ever wanted to do between my other pursuits was to play with my Barbie, plaiting her hair and getting her dressed up in her different outfits.

My mum, who was apparently a real tomboy when she was a child and not in the least bit interested in girlie things, used to give me an old-fashioned look sometimes and say, 'Katherine, I really don't know where you came from.' But that's how it was. I just have very feminine tastes. To this day, I don't mind going to the gym and doing a good workout and I love watching a game of rugby, but that aside I don't play any sports. As part of our PE sessions at school, we occasionally had dance sessions, when we'd choreograph routines and then perform them, and I loved that; but when it came to cross-country, running up the mountains, no way; netball, forget it (I worried about breaking a nail); hockey, not me. I hated all that.

For me, my best-ever memories always seem to stem from being with the people I love, enjoying each other's company, having a laugh. We're a big family when we all get together. My mum's twin sister, Louise, has two children—Gavin, who's five years older than me, and Melanie who's three years older. Mum's younger sister, Jo, has three girls: Naomi, Hannah and Ruth. Then there's her brother, my uncle Chris, who has two boys, Grifydd and Denzil, who are the eldest offspring in the family. All in all, including my godmothers and their children, our family makes a group of about twenty. I have a wonderful memory, when I was about eleven, of us all going together to Pembrey Park, a beautiful country park. It had a dry ski slope, a miniature train, an adventure playground and a beautiful beach. The highlight of the day,

18

though, was when we decided to make a massive Mickey Mouse out of all the things we could find on the beach. We'd seen this done on *Blue Peter*, and we all had such fun scavenging for pebbles, shells and seaweed.

This has reminded me that one of my mum's favourite memories of my childhood stems from when I was about four years old and had been amusing myself by collecting pebbles on the beach. I was very keen and had collected so many I couldn't carry them all in my hands, so I started posting them inside my bikini bottoms. Mum and Dad could see me waddling up the beach towards them, with my lumpy bikini bottoms threatening to fall down around my ankles, and when I finally made it to them, feeling proud of my efforts, they were in hysterics. I always was an enthusiastic child.

Even though Neath is an old market town that is big enough to have three comprehensive schools, everyone feels that they know everyone. When I walk across the small town centre, for example, it can take at least half an hour because there are so many familiar faces to stop and talk to. I guess, too, we Jenkins have always been very social people who are active within the community. Mum, for example, was on the Parent Teacher Association for the school, as well as a member of the church council and tennis club; and, from seven up, as I said, Laura and I were in the church choir, the choir club and then the Girl Guides, so we ended up knowing everyone.

Neath is the kind of place where it's good to grow up, where everybody looks after each other. I loved where I lived but I wasn't ever really tempted to play out in the streets or wander too far afield. I was aware, of course, that there was a park right at the back of our house, where all the kids loved to play and be out and about on their bikes, but I never wanted to do that. I liked structured activities and loved having something on the go every night of the week. So what has changed? What's new? Nothing. And I couldn't be happier.

Way back then, though, in 1990, something truly momentous was about to happen; something that would change my life forever and determine the direction my future would take—and I had only just reached the grand old age of ten.

THREE

SONGBIRD

There are some moments in life you never forget and receiving the letter telling me I had won a place in the Welsh Choir Girl of the Year competition was definitely one of these. I could not have been more excited.

This had come about because some weeks earlier, at the end of an evening's choir practice, the choir master had singled out me and a couple of other young choristers and told us he was going to enter us for the competition.

'What do we have to do for that?' we quizzed him excitedly.

'Continue to work hard,' he replied.

We were all ready to do that.

At this time the Welsh Choir Girl of the Year competition was sponsored by BET, a cleaning company, and in order to enter, we each had to make an individual recording, singing either a hymn or an anthem of our choice. I had no difficulty deciding what I'd like to sing—a piece by Wesley called 'Love One Another' that we always sang at weddings. I have a very distinct memory of where we recorded this: it was in one of the priest's seats, the seats where they sit when taking services, and the recording just consisted of me singing, accompanied by an organ. I was more elated than nervous to be making my very first recording and really pleased when everybody seemed happy with the result.

21

A few weeks later, when the all-important letter arrived to tell me and another chorister that our entry had been successful and we had made it to the Welsh finals that were to be held in St Mary's Church, Cardiff, I was beside myself with excitement. We were also informed that television cameras would be present and the finals would be featured on the Welsh television news. For this event, I had to choose two pieces to sing and I decided to go with a suggestion from Mum: The 'Nunc Dimittis' from the TV series *Tinker, Tailor, Soldier, Spy* along with the anthem 'O Taste and See'.

I loved the whole experience. Competition aside, it was always a thrill to go on a family outing to Cardiff, the biggest city in Wales. It is a vibrant city that is awash in music and talent. Dame Shirley Bassey, famous for her big voice and now considered Wales's first lady of song, came from Cardiff Bay (often called Tiger Bay); the author Roald Dahl; sports folk Colin Jackson and Dame Tanni Grey-Thompson; and singer Charlotte Church—all come from Cardiff.

On the day of the competition, I travelled to Cardiff with Joanne, another chorister from our church, and Mum, Dad and Laura. Some of her friends came along, too. After all the entrants had had their moment and sung before the three judges and the congregation in St Mary's, there was a break for adjudication. Then, while we entrants all held our breath and sat searching the sea of faces, the name of the winner, the girl who was Welsh Choir Girl of the Year, was announced. It was not me. It was another songbird, a girl who really deserved to win. She was about fifteen years old—

22

and I was totally in awe of her because she had such a lovely, mature voice. I had barely recovered from the excitement of clapping her until my hands tingled when I heard my name announced. I had come second and, looking at Mum's, Dad's and Laura's faces, which were ecstatic, my joy soared upwards and through the roof of the church. True to their word, the final was covered by the Welsh News.

I'd got the bug and could hardly bear to wait twelve months to repeat the experience. I was fired up, willing to practise harder than ever to ensure a place in the next contest and, with a little bit of luck, get my hands on that Choir Girl of the Year title.

*   *   *

As mentioned, I had learned to sing from the age of seven in the church choir of St David's, Neath, where the choir master, Howell Price, set a very high standard and worked us hard—at least one practice a week and two Sunday services—and all that held me in very good stead. Howell, a man who had a vocation to pass on his love of choral music to others, was only too happy to give young members of the choir extra practice and tuition in reading music. He also helped us to get over any nerves by encouraging us to sing solo in front of each other.

Nothing dampened my enthusiasm. I loved singing and when, at the age of ten, there was a big shake-up and a number of people left the choir, I was overjoyed to be made head chorister. It was also around that time, just as I was coming up to

23

eleven, that Mum and Dad got me my own singing teacher, Wyn Evans, as a reward for my always wanting to work so hard.

Dressing up for services and special occasions was, of course, part and parcel of being in the choir. For services, we always donned the traditional, full-length blue cassock and white surplice with a white ruff around the neck. According to the awards we won, we wore medals with different coloured ribbons that ranged from light blue, dark blue, red to two special green and purple ones, which were awarded only to those who went away to do an exam. I can't remember a time when I wasn't working towards my next ribbon.

In between all this activity we sang at weddings. I loved singing at these and really enjoyed seeing the church decked out in flowers, the bride arrive in the church doorway then walk down the aisle to the joyful strains of the 'Wedding March'. Weddings are such joyous occasions and some of the dresses were to die for. The other bonus, aside from these visual delights, was that we were paid £2 a wedding; one particular Saturday we had a record four weddings in one day and I trotted home with £8 tucked safely in my pocket and a huge grin on my face.

One way or another, the year between my first Welsh Choir Girl of the Year final and the next soon passed and, in 1991, I once again made my tape and got myself entered into the contest. I soon learned that this time five other choristers from our church would be going through to the final, as well as myself, which meant I would be competing against quite a few of my friends. A year earlier, at the age of ten, I had become a member of the

Royal School of Church Music (RSCM) Cathedral Singers, with my eyes set on the possibility of one day achieving the St Cecilia Award, its highest accolade. (Between 1994 and 1997, I was also a member of the National Youth Choir of Wales.)

These days, whenever parents say to me, 'My daughter wants to be a singer, what do you advise?' my mind always goes back to those days, and I always say: She should immerse herself in as much music as possible; she should join a local, county or national choir, and attend things like the Royal School of Church Music (RSCM) Cathedral Singers. There are so many opportunities on offer that it really is a question of making the most of all of them because all these experiences will make her a better musician.

Being a member of the National Youth Choir of Wales and attending its summer courses every year provided me with some of the best fun I've ever had; and I made two friends there, Katie Durling and Jane Tomlinson, who are still two of my best friends today. The choir changed its conductors every three years but I have never forgotten Ralph Alwood, who was a great inspiration.

I also recommend parents to encourage youngsters to enter competitions. I entered loads and didn't always win, but they all provided me with good experience and I learned something from each of them.

I've just remembered that in those days, I was prone to trying out things that I was convinced would help my voice. During the Welsh Choir Girl of the Year in 1991, I became convinced that if I sucked a lemon, it would improve my voice. I have this vivid memory of my mum chopping up countless lemons and putting all the pieces in a glass with ice, so I could just sit in a chair, screw up my face because they were so bitter, and suck all the juice out of them. I don't know what on earth I was thinking. Firstly, all that acid and the cold ice cubes constricts and tightens the muscles of the throat, which is the last thing you need to happen when you are singing. I would never suck lemons now, but at the time I was convinced sucking them made a difference.

Once again, for the Welsh Choir Girl of the Year contest, I chose to sing two pieces and, on that afternoon, oblivious to everything but the sound of my voice echoing around the church, I sang my heart out. The truth is that whatever contest or competition I entered, I always felt that this was my one and only chance, a chance that might never come again for me to prove myself. And, today, whenever I step into a room or on to a stage, I am still the same.

There was a break for the adjudicators to make their decision and every finalist and their choirmasters, families and friends held their breath. When I heard my name announced, it took a few seconds for what was being said to sink in, and I remember looking at Mum, Dad and Laura for reassurance. They were beaming and Mum threw her arms around me. But, yes, I had heard correctly. It was true. I had won. I was Welsh Choir Girl of the Year.

There are no words to describe a moment like that. I'd been elated and overjoyed when I came second the previous year, but now I'd come first and was going to London for the national finals, which were to be held at St George's, Hanover

Square—a famous church with a very strong choral tradition, where Handel was once a regular worshipper.

That event, though, turned out to be a really nerve-racking, tummy-churning experience—and not because of pre-performance nerves. Nothing to do with that. I was downstairs in the vestry when all of a sudden huge dogs and their handlers appeared from nowhere. They were police dogs and their handlers were police officers. There had been a bomb threat—a bomb threat at the National Finals of the Choir Girl of the Year, for goodness' sake. But it wasn't really so surprising. This was 1991, the year when, in an attempt to assassinate Prime Minister John Major, the IRA (Irish Republican Army) launched a mortar bomb that landed in the garden of No. 10 Downing Street. That night, though, I was completely freaked out by the police dogs straining at their leashes and, although the evening passed without further ado, I don't think I sang very well that night and didn't make it into the top three places.

This blip did not stop the bookings coming in for my first professional jobs, however. Every little village in Wales has a male voice choir that puts on annual concerts and, once I'd entered and won the Welsh Choir Girl of the Year competition, I started to get regular invitations to go along to these as the guest soloist. I was thrilled to be asked to sing, and to be earning some money. For these events I was sometimes paid £10, sometimes £20. I didn't have an agent or anything like that in those days. All my bookings came about by word of mouth. Somebody who knew somebody would give out Mum's telephone number and they'd call her. Even at that age, I was careful with the money I earned and always invested it back into my singing—such as buying a new dress for my next concert. Then, from about the age of thirteen onwards, I also got bookings to sing at weddings as a soloist. So, from a very young age, I was kind of professional and never lacked employment.

*   *   *

I met the girl who was to become my all-time best friend on the first day I entered the classroom of my comprehensive school, aged eleven. Her name was Kristy and I noticed her at once because she had an amazing head of long, blonde hair.

'Can I sit next to you?' I remember asking her, precisely at the same moment as she said, 'Can I sit next to you?' Somehow in that moment, I knew we would be best friends for life; and we have been ever since. We have always been very much alike and have always been very good at motivating each other. The fact that we succeeded in staying together in the same class throughout our senior schooldays was thanks to my mum.

At the end of the first year in school, which pupils spent in mixed-ability groups, we were then re-sorted into sets when the first lot of exam results came through. Within these sets, there were three classes for the top set and, although both Kristy and I qualified for this, we were, to our dismay, put into different classes. I was so upset when I found out that Mum decided to call the school to see if anything could be done.

'I actually think these two girls are good for each other,' she said. 'They motivate each other to work hard, so if there is anything that can be done . . . '

There was. To our great relief, the school moved us into the same class, and there we remained for the remainder of our schooldays. And, no doubt about it, we were good for each other. Kristy always knew that she wanted to be a doctor and when you have a friend who wants to work hard, who remains true to what they want to do, you, too, are motivated to work hard. I've always been incredibly proud of Kristy, who, against all odds after she lost her mum to cancer at the beginning of the fifth year of school, still managed to remain focused and succeeded in becoming a doctor. Dr Kristy Mellin, your mum would be so proud.

*   *   *

During my childhood, Mum and Dad bought a caravan and the four of us used to go off on the most wonderful, adventurous touring holidays. Sometimes, during the long school holidays, we'd set off and explore the different regions of France. Then at weekends, at least eight times a year, we'd go away with family friends who also had a caravan. Sometimes these travels might take us only six miles down the road. That didn't matter. It was always fun to get away and spend time together. Dad would get out the barbecue and the smell of burgers and hot dogs would fill the air. In the evenings, Dad would be his usual hilarious self, reducing us all to hysterics, or we'd just sit around and have brilliant fun playing 'Newmarket', a game of chance with cards. For this we'd play for pistachio shells. We were, you can tell, really hardened gamblers in our family.

Although by now I had entered my teens, I guess I didn't kick over all the traces and do many of the crazy things that teenagers do; and I certainly wasn't one for hanging around my bedroom, playing music at the kind of volume that drives parents doolally. In fact, I hardly listened to pop music, not because I didn't like it, but because I was too busy doing my own things. I do remember some of the music that was in the charts during my teenage years and, I am almost ashamed to say now, I remember loving an American boy band called New Kids on the Block.

My older cousin, Melanie, was into pop and she really influenced me and Laura. But, although I sometimes watched things like *Top of the Pops,* I never really got to screaming pitch about any group in particular and never ventured out to gigs and concerts or felt compelled to write a fan letter.

The first song I ever bought was Madonna's 'Material Girl'; but it wasn't so much the song or her voice that made me buy this; it was the video that captured my imagination. I thought it was the most glamorous video I had ever seen. Madonna, with her blonde hair, diamonds and pink dress, was just like my idol, Marilyn Monroe: so glamorous, just how I wanted to be. I would sing that song constantly and even now certain things like dresses and jewellery make me say 'I'm having a "Material Girl" moment.'

From about fifteen onwards, I did start to take more of an interest in really strong female vocalists, whose rendering of songs was full of heartfelt emotion and passion, and I particularly loved the incredible voices of Whitney Houston singing 'The Greatest Love of All' and 'I Will Always Love

You'; Judy Garland's 'The Man That Got Away'; Dolly Parton's 'Jolene' and 'Nine to Five'; Mariah Carey's 'Without You'; Barbra Streisand's 'People' and Jennifer Rush's 'The Power Of Love'.

Despite this, however, it never crossed my mind to be a pop singer and I don't think I would have made a good one, even though when I was very young and people asked me what I wanted to be, I always replied, 'I want to be a pop star.' When I said this, I didn't really understand what 'pop star' meant, I just knew I wanted to be a singer.

In truth, though, I was always more inspired by classical than pop music. For example, I always loved Maria Callas. My admiration for her wasn't so much for the voice itself, but for the level of emotion and commitment she injected into her singing. I also found the stories about her life fascinating. I've always thought of her as opera's diva and I love listening to her recordings for the sheer intensity of her passion.

Likewise, I have always loved Pavarotti and Placido Domingo, who both have something very special in their voices. Some singers can be technically perfect, but there is still something lacking, but for me, Pavarotti and Domingo have an extra dimension that cannot be created. It is either there or not. It's a certain attribute, tone, that connects the singer with the listeners and releases the emotions of both. Pavarotti had this, Domingo has it and Andrea Bocelli has it.

I must say I've also always had a very special place in my heart for Domingo, Carreras and Pavarotti as the 'Three Tenors'. They were the first crossover artists, and the first to take classical music to the World Cup.

*   *   *

The third and final time I represented Wales at the Choir Girl of the Year competition was in 1994, when I was fourteen. By this time the BET Competition had finished and the BBC had set up their own one. If I remember rightly, we didn't know about the competition in 1992, and in 1993 they didn't select my tape for the final. On this occasion I remember my mum coming up to the school, clutching a letter with the BBC logo printed on the envelope. She couldn't bear to open it—and couldn't bear to wait for me to come home to open it. When, with trembling fingers, I did, I discovered that I had made it through to the national finals, which, this time, were being held at Manchester Town Hall.

I never actually succeeded in winning the national title. The girl who did in 1994 was Tabitha Watling, who went on to study at the Royal College of Music, London, and we still know each other. Disappointed though I was not to win the national competition, I still appreciated the fact that it had all been incredibly good experience and that taking part in it had introduced me to many inspiring people I would not otherwise have met.

Such competitions really are an opportunity to learn. You are given time to talk to the judges and find out what you need to do to improve your singing; and you learn the value of constructive criticism. I was very sensitive in those days and often took criticism too personally, but gradually I began to appreciate that that is how I could improve and learn to do better, and by the time I'd been through several terms at the Royal Academy of Music and survived so many singing lessons in which I was constantly told what to do to improve, I'd become immune to criticism, but just accepted it as the only way to make progress.

After I won Welsh Choir Girl of the Year, people kept mistaking Laura for me and when they came up to her and clasped her hand and said, 'I think you sang so well', Laura, without batting an eyelid, would reply, 'Thank you *very* much.' She's always had a very dry sense of humour.

After winning the Welsh Choir Girl of the Year competition, various articles were published about me in local and national Welsh papers, making my name quite well known in my area, so I got even more singing engagements at weddings and numerous male voice choirs started inviting me to sing with them. Wales, as everybody knows, is famous for its male voice choirs, and the last I heard they numbered over a thousand. In the early days the choirs drew their membership from local mining and slate-quarry villages, but nowadays the singers come from a multitude of occupations and include professors, plumbers, computer consultants, television producers, barmen, firemen, farmers and bankers—anyone who shares a love of music and singing is welcome in the male voice choirs.

If anybody was worried about my spending so much time in the company of so many charming, talented men, whose voices filled the Welsh valleys, they need not have been. By then, aged fourteen, I had met Kevin, my first boyfriend, and I was already in love and spoken for. Kevin was in the year above me at school and was always one of a

33

group of boys whom I thought were by far the best-looking ones. The first time I saw him I thought, 'Oh gosh, he's so handsome—*gorg-eous*'. He had jet-black hair, was about 5ft 10in, with perfect olive skin that always looked sun-tanned, and a very handsome face with a lovely smile. Then when we were doing the school production of *Calamity Jane*, in which I was playing Katie and he was playing one of the minor male parts, I discovered he was also a lovely person, too. It was during the rehearsals for *Calamity Jane* that we got to know each other, and it was at one of the dress rehearsals that he plucked up his courage and asked me to go out with him.

I was so shy when it came to boys. I had never had a boyfriend and, not really knowing what to say and how to react, I said, 'Oh, Kevin, I'm going to have to think about it.' I was serious. I went away and really gave it some deep thought, then talked to my friends about it. 'Are you crazy?' all the girls said. 'What's to think about? He's absolutely *gorg-eous.*' So, the next time I saw Kevin, I said, 'Yes.'

I know it sounds silly, but within a day we were head-over-heels in love, and I can't think of a single bad thing to say about him. He was one of the nicest and most caring people you could ever hope to meet and I came to love his family like my own. Kevin remained my boyfriend for six years. I really couldn't have wished for a more perfect first love and it is because of him that I know that true love is pure, honest and unconditional.

*   *   *

Music was obviously always my favourite subject at

school, but I also really enjoyed history lessons, which, at my comprehensive school, were taken by a fantastic teacher called Mrs Handley, a warm, talented teacher, who was so encouraging that her pupils always wanted to learn what she was teaching them.

Mrs Howells and Mrs Brown were my music teachers and both were infinitely generous with their time, always taking us for extra-curricular activities, such as after-school choir practice, running orchestras and helping Mrs Good, my drama teacher, put on the end-of-term shows.

As well as being chosen to play the part of Katie in *Calamity Jane*, I was given the lead part of Adelaide in *Guys and Dolls* when I was fifteen; and it was when I was in the middle of rehearsing for this that disaster struck!

Just two weeks before the show, I went down with a very nasty case of glandular fever. Luckily I knew my part off by heart and the school let me take time off from all my lessons to help me recuperate in time for the big night. Glandular fever leaves you feeling incredibly exhausted and run down. The only way I could cope when I went in for the last few rehearsals was to eat one of those huge bars of Cadbury's milk chocolate (something I would never do now) to give me the energy I needed. Some of us really suffer for our art! I wouldn't have missed *Guys and Dolls*—or the chocolate—for the world.

To be given the chance to learn and hone my stagecraft in productions such as those while still at school was just *fab-lous*; and it wasn't until I left school that I realised teachers don't get paid for coaching kids in all those extra-curricular activities.

I'm so thankful to Mrs Howells, Mrs Brown and Mrs Good for giving us so many creative opportunities.

My next project was to work towards my St Cecilia Award, the Royal School of Church Music's highest honour. It really was hard work, involving a lot of preparation of pieces to sing, plus a written exam that included questions about the church's calendar and festivals, and the colours of the altar cloths to coincide with the calendar. When I learned I had achieved the award, it made all the hard work worthwhile. The actual presentation, I was told, was to be conducted by a bishop—always considered a very special honour—and the big occasion was to take place at Llandaff Cathedral, Cardiff.

I was so thrilled that day and so proud of my award, even more so because Mum, Dad, Laura and Nanna, as well as most of my aunties and uncles, were there, which really made it a great family occasion and day out. Life was so good— doors kept opening and I just kept walking through them.

The actual award consisted of a medal, which was to be worn thereafter whenever I donned my choirgirl's cassock and surplice. The medal itself was on a red ribbon and replaced, with one exception, all the other colours I'd been awarded in the past. By then, I'd been made head chorister and the one exception meant that I was able to wear the St Cecilia medal with my head chorister's ribbon.

After that success, all I wanted to do was re-double my efforts and I never resented a single moment I gave to my singing studies. As well as remaining a member of the National Youth Choir of Wales until 1997, I continued to concentrate on my Royal School of Music singing exams, which I took up to Grade Eight, and then worked my way through the various examination grades for piano.

Singing 'I'm going down the garden to eat worms' at school had a lot to answer for. Winning that talent contest at the age of four clinched matters for me; and having gone on to learn the 'Teapot' and the 'Banana' songs, I never looked back, remaining totally immersed in my singing thereafter. I didn't know it then, of course, but, one day, not so very far off in the scheme of things, I would find myself sitting here writing a chapter of this book and thinking, 'Yes, big things have small beginnings'—and nobody could be more appreciative of that fact than I am.

And so it seemed that my life was full of happiness and laughter. It was, but it was not to last. Unbeknown to Mum, Dad, Laura and me, a catastrophe had been lurking in the wings of our lives; one that would break our hearts and shatter our lives.

FOUR

O, MY BELOVED FATHER

The news could not have been more devastating. Dad, we were told, had lung cancer. Apart from keeping him as comfortable as possible, nothing more could be done.

We were all in shock. We had known Dad wasn't feeling well, that he had gone to see the doctor because he had developed a persistent cough that he just couldn't shake off, but we had no idea it was anything more serious than a smoker's cough. By the age of fifteen, having seen Kristy lose her mum to cancer, I knew what cancer meant; knew that this was a word—an illness—that struck fear and dread into people's hearts.

'We have to stay strong for each other,' Mum kept telling Laura and me as she struggled to contain her own emotions. But how do you stay strong when the person you love best in the whole world is suffering and your heart is in pieces?

Until then, Dad had always been such an exuberant, larger-than-life character, always ready with a joke or comic turn of phrase. I had not fully appreciated that he was nearly seventy years old; and I couldn't accept that there might come a time when he might not always be there.

The doctors and cancer specialist were honest: they told Mum the truth in the kindest way they knew how. When the time came for Mum to tell Laura and me she, in turn, was equally honest and did not try to soften the blow by feeding us half-truths and raising false hopes. Nobody, we were told, could be absolutely sure, but it would probably be just a matter of months before we would have to say our goodbyes. For his sake we had to make the most of his last few months and make things as easy as we could for him.

Living as we did in a small tight-knit community, everybody rallied around and nobody could do enough to help Dad or us, something we'll never forget. I must say, though, that however much Mum and Dad had tried to cover up for our sakes, I knew Dad wasn't well. Even before Mum told us, I could tell he wasn't himself. He and Mum, for example, always used to go out on Saturday nights, but they had stopped going because Dad was not feeling up to it and kept saying he had a headache. Then, one day when I was in my bedroom, I heard him coming upstairs and could hear what an effort this was for him. He was huffing and puffing and obviously struggling and I knew it wasn't a good sign. I'd never known him to be that sick before and I'm sure, looking back, that Dad had been diagnosed with lung cancer by then, but they were trying to keep it from Laura and me for as long as possible.

Then came the dreadful Sunday when Mum decided we had to be told. Our routine on Sundays was morning service at our local church, home about midday to lay the table for the lovely roast dinner that Dad always cooked for us, then after lunch we'd all go off and do our own thing. Sometimes I would go out with the family for an afternoon walk, but more usually in those days I'd go over to see Kevin and spend the afternoon with him, before returning home at 5.30 p.m. to go to

Evensong.

On the Sunday that Mum told us the awful news, I was in the bedroom with Laura, getting ready to go and see Kevin. 'I have to talk to you both,' she began . . . then she told us that Dad had lung cancer and was too upset to tell us this himself. He was, Mum added, very embarrassed and disappointed because he felt he was letting us all down very badly. She told us that the consultant thought it was only going to be a matter of months before he died. Everything she said after that remains a blur. All I remember is the three of us crying our hearts out, then I went round to cry on Kevin's shoulder.

Everyone at school was really understanding. Huw and the other teachers kept saying, 'If you need some time off, Katherine, that's fine.' But this was mid-March and my GCSEs started in May.

Dad had always smoked and, when he was diagnosed with lung cancer, he continued to smoke. One day, I got really upset about this and had a go at him: 'Why are you still smoking?' I asked, angrily. 'You've got lung cancer, Dad.'

'Katherine,' Mum said later, when she was having a quiet word with me, 'smoking's not going to make any difference to your dad now. If it makes him happy, let him smoke.'

I found this very hard to accept. Dad had smoked from a very young age, all through our childhood, but this was at a time when people were not really aware of the dangers of passive smoking. Even so, Laura and I had a gut feeling that smoking wasn't good for you and we used to tell off Dad and Mum. Neither Laura nor I have ever smoked, and Mum gave up after Dad died.

40

While he was sick, but still at home, Dad had had his seventieth birthday and, although it was painful because we knew it would be his last birthday, we managed a kind of party for him. I still was in denial and kept hoping he would get better. It wasn't to be though. In a matter of weeks we had to get used to our home becoming a kind of hospital, with District and Macmillan nurses coming in and out until Dad was taken into a special cancer hospice in Morriston, Swansea. I knew what it meant. Kristy's mum had passed away there just a few months earlier, and I found it so distressing to go and visit Dad in a place where I knew that people went to die. I was heartbroken.

Dad had always been so supportive of my schoolwork and my singing, but I felt really guilty about concentrating on revising while he was so ill. When I went to see him, thoughts about my exams were never far away and I was conscious that I needed to get home as soon as I could to get on with all my revision. On one of these occasions, I remember Dad looking at me and saying—and it breaks my heart to think of it—'You're just like me, Kath, you hate hospitals, you can't wait to get out of them.' My worrying about anything other than Dad at such a time has remained a huge regret, and if I could have that time over again I'd spend so much more time with him. Dad did come home again for a while, but when the pain became too bad, he had to go back into the hospice.

I was in school, in Mrs Ridge's biology class, when a school secretary came to the door and said, 'Katherine, your Auntie Jo is here. You have to go home immediately.' I knew then, of course, that something terrible was happening, but I was

41

shocked because it had only been a matter of weeks, not months. When I walked along the school corridor, Auntie Jo was standing there, looking distraught. She took me into the office, sat me down, and said, 'Katherine, your dad is in a coma and you need to go to see him.' By the time we arrived at Tŷ Olwen, the hospice, they had moved Dad from the ward to a family room, a special little unit that was like a self-contained flat with its own kitchen, living-room with sofa-beds and, of course, a room for Dad.

All this happened on the Wednesday before I was due to leave school for the last time for study leave on the Friday; and Mum, Laura and I stayed there with Dad for two days. All day on the Wednesday, members of the family kept coming in and out to visit him; but even then, I really didn't think the end was going to come so quickly. I was fifteen, in denial, immature, thinking about school, about the hall that had been booked for the leaving party on Friday night, about what we were going to wear, who my friends were going with—that sort of stuff—and it seemed strange not to be a part of it, to think I wouldn't be there for my last day ever at school.

I was so overwrought I couldn't sleep the first night, and when a nurse came in to check on Dad, she could see my distress and said, 'You know, although your dad is in a coma, he can hear you. If you go in and talk to him, he will hear what you say, even though he can't respond.' So I took over from Mum, who was exhausted, and went into his room and sat there, holding his hand. Then, between sobs, I managed to tell him how much I loved him; that he'd been the best ever father, everything I could have wished for. I had so needed that chance to talk to him, and to this day I am grateful to that nurse for telling me he could hear me.

At about four o'clock the next day, 2 May 1995, my Auntie Jo came into the room where Laura and I were and said she was taking us home to give us something to eat, then we could come back. I was pretty sure Mum knew what was about to happen and wanted to minimise the distress for us, and I really didn't want to go. At the same time I didn't want to upset Mum any more than she was already. So, very reluctantly, I went with Laura to Auntie Jo's, and she made us a pizza. All I could think about as I was pretending to eat was that I wanted to go back. 'Can we go now? I really want to go back now,' I kept nagging Auntie Jo.

As we pulled up in the car outside the hospice, I knew we were too late. As I ran down the hospice corridor, I saw Mum, and everyone else who was there, in tears. Dad had just passed away.

I've heard people say since then that when someone is dying they sometimes wait for the least painful moment for their loved ones before passing on, and Dad clearly thought that this was the right moment for him to leave Laura and me. I was devastated, but because I knew how much pain he had been in, it was a kind of release. I decided at that moment that I would be the strong one now for Mum and Laura's sake.

After lots of tears and hugs from my family, Mum asked us if we wanted to go in and see Dad one last time. She added that she thought it was best that we didn't, that the last picture we had of him was a nice one, but I was adamant. I knew instinctively that I would need this kind of closure, and I am so glad I insisted on it. It was not a scary experience, far from it. During his illness Dad had looked much older, so deathly pale, and had lost so much weight that he was horrifically thin and gaunt at the end. But when I saw him after he had passed away, he looked really well again. The colour had come back to this face and hair, and he looked as he hadn't looked for ages; and that was very comforting.

The next day, the Friday, knowing that this was what Dad would have wanted and expected of me, I went to school and managed to keep myself together. I didn't cry because I knew that if the tears started to flow, they would never stop. Later, while the school-leaving party was in progress, my head of year, Mrs Davies, came over and said, 'How are you doing, Katherine?'

'Fine, really,' I replied, choked.

'I'll see you on Wednesday, then,' she said.

'Wednesday? What's on Wednesday?' I queried.

'The funeral. Didn't they tell you?' she asked, surprised. I shook my head.

I hadn't been told and it really upset me. Each time, it seemed, other people knew what was happening before I did. But this wasn't intentional. It just happened that way. Mum, I understand with hindsight, was totally grief-stricken and was doing the best she could. At such times there are bound to be things that cause resentment and, at that moment, I was very angry with her. Both Laura and I were dealing with the grief in our own ways, but because Laura dealt with hers so privately and silently, I worried about her and felt even more protective towards her.

When we were getting ready for the funeral, I

remember Nanna telling me I wasn't to wear much make-up and, really angry with her, I thought, 'Is that really important today?' I was a teenager who no longer wanted to be told what to do all the time, and I thought I should be able to dress and do whatever I thought was right.

The funeral was held at St David's, the biggest church in Neath, which can hold over a thousand people, where I did all my singing. It was packed when we walked in, and I was completely overwhelmed that so many teachers and friends from school had come to show their respect.

Both Laura and I felt so strongly that we wanted to do something special for Dad's funeral. I knew that I would be too distraught to sing on the day, so we decided to record a piece with me singing 'Pie Jesu', a requiem that was one of Dad's favourites, with Laura accompanying me on the organ. When this was played at the service, it seems the whole congregation was reduced to tears. Afterwards people kept coming up to us and telling us how emotional that part of the service had been.

As we walked down the aisle to go to the crematorium, I was so devastated I couldn't look anybody in the eye. Then, as I got into the car, I turned round to see my poor friend, Kristy, being supported by two teachers. I'd never seen anybody so distraught. The funeral had brought back the death of her mother, and all I wanted to do was get out of the car and run to her, but Kevin placed a gentle hand on my arm and I knew for Mum's and Laura's sake I couldn't.

For days after the funeral I was so upset that Dad and I had never really talked about what was happening to him, but at the time I knew that he

45

thought he was letting us all down and I was afraid that if I showed him how devastated I was, this would make him feel even worse. The last time I saw him, when he was still conscious, on the men's ward at Tŷ Olwen, I said, as I left, 'I'm really hoping you'll get better, Dad'; and this was the only direct reference I ever made to his being ill. It was such a stupid thing to say, and I could have kicked myself for saying it. Afterwards I was haunted by the fact that he knew he wasn't going to get better and I thought saying 'get better' must have made it so much worse for him. That was the last thing I ever said to him and it must have tortured him.

Within a few days of the funeral, my exams started. The first was the French oral, then a week after that all the other exams began. What helped me to get through these was an extraordinary experience I had the night before my maths exam, when Dad came to me in a dream. Because Dad was always at home and Mum was out at work, he was the one I always went to when I needed help with my school work; thankfully, the one thing he was really good at was maths, which was not my best subject. Aware of that, he had always sat down and helped me come to grips with any equation I was finding difficult. The night before my maths exam I was convinced, never having been a last-minute person, that I'd done all the studying and revising I needed to do, and I was glad to climb into the bottom bunk of our bunk beds. Underneath these were several big plastic storage boxes where I kept all my school books.

At about five o'clock that morning, I awoke from a vivid dream in which my dad was saying, 'Look under the bed, love. Look under the bed.' Suddenly

46

wide awake, I climbed out of bed and did as Dad had instructed, and there, to my surprise, was a maths notebook in which I had written just one thing—an algebra equation on the first page of the book. I was such a swot that to find a book, albeit one page of a book, that I hadn't studied filled me with dread. So I sat there and studied it, then went back to bed.

The next day, the day of the maths exam, I turned over the last page of the examination paper and there, unbelievably, was an algebra question that needed the equation I had read that morning. For me, there was absolutely no doubt in my mind that this had been Dad's way of telling me he was okay, still a part of my life and still able to help me. When I came out of the hall after completing the exam, all the other kids were saying 'Oh, my God, wasn't that last question solid.' I got an 'A' for that exam.

People can say that they don't believe in things like that, and I agree such events do sound bizarre, but that's exactly what happened. I am sure that for me the drive to succeed came from knowing that Dad had put so much of his time and energy into me; and, to this day, I am always saying to myself, 'I want to do this for you, Dad, as well as for me.'

I was actually okay while I had the exams to focus on, but when these finished I had the long summer to face when, basically, I was left to my own devices and could do whatever I wanted. It was during this time that I started to have bad nightmares. I kept dreaming that Dad was back at home, that burglars had broken into the house and he was too sick to defend himself and us; or that the house was on fire and, as he was too sick to help himself, it was up to me to get him out. I used to wake up in pools of sweat and, in the end, I was too frightened to go to sleep and couldn't sleep at all. Mum, who had already received some bereavement counselling, suggested that I should go too but I was a stroppy teenager and refused to go.

However, when the nightmares continued and got even worse, I felt I had no option but to change my mind and I'm so glad I did. The counselling really helped and was the best thing I could have done at that time. Until then, I hadn't really talked to an adult about what I was going through, or told anyone that I was feeling really weird—angry and resentful—towards my mum; and I was also able to mention how pained I felt about not really having had a heart-to-heart with Dad and said a proper goodbye. 'You must write him a letter,' the counsellor said, 'a letter in which you put down all the things you wished you had said.' And I did; and it really helped. I still have that letter, but I have not been able to re-read it since.

At one level, although we had lost Dad, I realised how extra-ordinarily fortunate Laura and I had been. Because Dad had always done so much for us, we had spent more time in his company than most children ever do with their fathers. But that also meant our closeness and our love had deepened throughout those years; and the closer you are and the more you love a person, the more you grieve when you lose them.

After Dad died, there were so many moments like that, moments when I found myself closing down, when I wanted to build a wall around my heart, pull up the drawbridge and withdraw into a safe haven where nobody could reach me. I can see now that playing safe, switching off, was my state of mind—or, perhaps, I should say the state of my heart—for some months after Dad died. I went through a horrible phase of being really bolshy with Mum. I know we tried to be there for each other, but we were going through completely different emotions. My mum's grief at losing the love of her life, and my grief at losing my dad, were two completely different things; and I didn't make it any easier for Mum by keeping her at arm's length and sharing everything instead with Kevin, who could not have been more supportive at that time. I justified this by thinking that Mum had her sisters to support her, but now I can see that I didn't really understand what she was going through, and I accept that my behaviour was very inconsiderate and hurtful.

With hindsight, and with a maturity that's been gained during the intervening years, I can see that my reactions then were a mixture of being a teenager who, like most teenagers, was suffering from the usual mood swings and misguided belief that I knew everything and was ready to call all my own shots and be independent, and working through my grief. It was just as if I had hardened my heart, become an empty vessel who could only feel for myself and cope with my own grief and suffering. I was angry with God for taking Dad, but took my anger out on Mum. I smiled, but didn't live in my smile. These days, thank God, I am no longer finding everything so hopeless, or arguing with Mum, or having a go at God; and I feel that Dad is still with me.

Something very strange occurred about nine

years after Dad died, when I appeared as a guest on a Living TV programme hosted by the medium, Colin Fry. In my goodbye letter to Dad, which nobody but me has ever read, I had mentioned Dad's love of cricket. 'I hope your heaven stretches across the whole wide world,' I had written, 'and that you drift being able to see all the cricket matches you want to see.' When Colin Fry was using his psychic talents on me, a lot of personal information came through, but the one thing that really stood out and got my attention was when he said, 'What's the link to Barbados?'

'There isn't one that I know of,' I replied.

'No, love, I'm sorry,' he continued, 'but this link is so strong I'm going to stick with it . . .'

'There is no link with Barbados . . .'

'No not Barbados,' he said suddenly. 'The West Indies. Your dad loved the cricket, didn't he?'

'Yes,' I gasped.

'Well, he wants you to know that he's watching the cricket.'

I could only gasp again. If I had wanted one sign that everything was okay with Dad, that would have been the one. Until that moment, I'd even forgotten that I'd written about cricket in my letter to him. I found that experience with Colin Fry very comforting, and it was a very reassuring confirmation of what I truly felt in my heart—that Dad was still with us.

In fact, the further I go on my chosen career path, the more certain I am that I am being guided by Dad, who was always such an inspiration. My belief in God is also strengthened by the comfort of knowing that he is still with me, conveying his feelings about things that I should and shouldn't

50

do. I particularly feel his presence every time I sing 'Do not stand at my grave and weep' because I know the words are so true of him. I have always treasured the words of this. Written by an unknown author, the poem goes:

> *Do not stand at my grave and weep*
> *I am not there*
> *I do not sleep*
> *I am a thousand winds that blow*
> *I am the diamond glint on snow.*
> *Do not stand at my grave and cry*
> *I am not there I did not die.*
> *I am the sunlight on ripened grain*
> *I am the gentle autumn rain*
> *When you wake in the morning's hush*
> *I am the swift uplifting rush*
> *of quiet birds in circled flight*
> *I am the soft stars that shine at night*
> *Do not stand at my grave and cry*
> *I am not there*
> *I did not die.*

This poem was apparently found by the parents of a soldier called Steve Cummins, who was killed while on active service in Northern Ireland. Obviously aware he might die in the conflict, he had copied the poem out by hand and left it in an envelope addressed to his mum and dad. I always have a struggle with my emotions when I sing this, but it is something I feel I have to do in honour of my Dad—and Steve Cummins.

Dad's birthday is at the beginning of April and, despite the passing of the years, I never forget his special day and make sure I call Mum and Laura on that day. Likewise, I always feel very close to him on the anniversary of his death. I am usually sensitive around this time and feel so raw. Sometimes I cry all day or just look at something and just burst into tears and be unable to stop myself. Likewise, when I first heard the Luther Vandross song, 'Dance with my father again' on my car radio, around the anniversary of Dad's death, I had to pull over because I couldn't stop crying. Time is a great healer, yes, but it can take plenty of time.

Much as I love it, I'm not at all sure that I will ever be able to sing Dido's lament, 'When I am laid in earth' because it has those heartbreaking lines, 'Remember Me'; and another song I find really hard to sing, which I seem to sing all the time now, is 'O Mio Babbino Caro'—'O, My Beloved Father'. The first time I sang this live was in 2006 at my concert to open the Eisteddfod at Llangollen and I dedicated it to my dad. 'We used to have a caravan and we came to this festival as a family when I was about ten,' I told the audience that night. 'My mum is here tonight, and I just know that Dad is here in spirit.'

In a way I wish I hadn't tried to sing 'O Mio Babbino Caro' live on that occasion because, when I did, I was so choked with emotion I don't think I sang it very well. The concert I did that night, though, was recorded and became my first DVD called *Katherine Jenkins Live at Llangollen*.

I love the fact that I'm in a position where I can dedicate all my albums to my dad. This makes it feel like he is on this amazing journey with me and I cherish keeping his memory alive in this way. I'm also glad when I get letters from people who say they have lost somebody and that they find strength and comfort in my music.

Losing Dad when we were so young couldn't have been more painful and difficult for Laura and me, and we both felt we had to grow up overnight. Because Dad was helped by the Macmillan nurses in the short time he had left, Laura decided to raise funds for them; being the mad, brave, adventurous person she is, she signed up to climb Mount Kilimanjaro in Tanzania, Africa's highest peak. Along with her friends, Michelle and Rachel, she raised over £16,000 by climbing it in five days in January 2007. I can't tell you how proud I was of her.

When I was a child I was forever singing to Dad, and now I'm grown up, I still sing for him. I'm utterly convinced he's listening and still guiding me through all the good fortune I have had. Before any big concert or event, when I know I really have to pull out all the stops, I turn to him and say, 'Come on, Dad, help me get through this one'; and he does—every time. That's the sort of man he was. Irreplaceable.

FIVE

RIGHT UP MY STREET

After Dad died—and particularly during the time I was being a bolshy teenager and giving my mum a hard time, it was my nanna who always tried to sort things out; who took on Dad's role and made Laura and me our tea when we came home from school and Mum was still at work.

Up until this period the church had always held an important place in my life, and both Laura and I had attended services since we were tiny. This was hardly surprising. Nanna had always been a pillar of the church and Mum taught at Sunday school. Our religion was Christian—Church in Wales to be exact—but I went right off God and religion when Kristy lost her young mum and I lost my dad soon after. It was all so cruel, so unfair and during that time I'm ashamed to say I lost my faith.

Since then, though, I've come to realise that these kind of reactions are very common following bereavement; that anger is part of loss and the easiest person to get angry with is God. During that time I came across the poem 'Footprints in the Sand', which I later discovered had been attributed to three authors, Mary Stevenson, Margaret Fishback Powers and Carolyn Carty, and I can't resist including the Mary Stevenson version here:

One night I dreamed I was walking along the beach with the Lord. Many scenes from my life flashed across the sky.

54

In each scene I noticed footprints in the sand. Sometimes there were two sets of footprints, other times there was only one.

This bothered me because I noticed that during the low periods of my life, when I was suffering from anguish, sorrow or defeat, I could see only one set of footprints, so I said to the Lord,

'You promised me, Lord, that if I followed you, you would walk with me always. But I have noticed that during the most trying periods of my life there has only been one set of footprints in the sand. Why, when I needed you most, have you not been there for me?'

The Lord replied, 'The years when you have seen only one set of footprints, my child, is when I carried you.'

Along with countless other people, I found this poem a great comfort. It summed up exactly how I was feeling. I'd felt that God had abandoned me, but then I realised he hadn't. So, in the end, my turning my back on Him proved to be only temporary. As I journeyed on through my teenage years, my faith returned and got even stronger, and I'm now a 'Friend of St David's in Neath'.

Despite our grief, Kristy and I, who were the only two people in our school year to lose a parent to cancer, still managed to gain 'A' grades in our GCSEs; and, as I remained quite sure that Dad would have wanted me to go on achieving whatever I was capable of, I decided to make the most of every moment. One event I treasure from that time was when the Pelenna Valley Male Voice Choir, with which I sang on a regular basis, granted me its scholarship grant of £250 for 'the most promising young singer'. I was so thrilled: and £250 was a huge amount of money, which I spent on music that I wanted to study.

When I was fourteen, I'd signed up for the Duke of Edinburgh Award scheme, which we were told would look really good on our CVs. Some of the benefits of this award, we were told, included developing self-confidence and self-reliance; gaining a sense of achievement and responsibility; discovering new interests and talents, and developing leadership skills and abilities. Just in case all this sounded too worthy to appeal to teenagers like us, we were also told we would make new friends, develop our communication, problem-solving and decision-making skills and have fun—plenty of fun!

There were, we were informed, three separate Duke of Edinburgh Awards that could be achieved—Bronze, Silver and Gold, and each of these involved work in four sections: Service, to encourage service to individuals and the community; Skills, to encourage the discovery and development of personal interest and social and practical skills; Physical Recreation, to encourage participation and improvement in physical activity; and Expeditions, to encourage a spirit of adventure and discovery.

Given my love of structured activities, all this was right up my street, and I really wanted to do it. So I did, and I was not disappointed. Having started the award scheme a year or so before Dad died, I just kept going after his death and achieved my awards.

For my community service, I ran a bingo night

for senior citizen ladies. I was what they called the 'bingo caller' and Laura came along to help out. I really enjoyed this, especially the squeals of excitement and the look of joy on the ladies' faces when they jigged up and down and called out *'Bingo!'* But after a few weeks, I had to stop taking Laura along as she kept winning all the prizes.

I had no idea when I was working towards my Bronze and Silver awards that one day the Duke of Edinburgh would ask me to assist him in presenting the current crop of awards. And what a satisfying thing that investiture proved to be. On these occasions, you get to visit either St James's Palace or Buckingham Palace where, in the rooms set aside for the investitures, the winners of the awards wait on one side of the room while two members of their family wait on the other side. In my room of award winners, I made what I hoped was an encouraging and inspiring speech, then the Duke of Edinburgh came in and, between us, we made a point of meeting and greeting everybody and handing out the certificates.

The first time I met the Duke of Edinburgh, I was introduced to him by an aide. 'Oh, yes,' he said as he came to rest by me. 'I think I've seen you singing at the rugby.' Then, as I smiled nervously, he added, 'How are your vocal cords, Katherine?'

'Oh, fine—fine, thank you,' I said breathlessly.

'No boils or warts on them yet?' he enquired.

I was absolutely horrified and said, 'I hope not.'

'Jolly good,' the Duke said, sauntering away.

These days, I attend the awards ceremony with him about once a year. I always write my own speeches for these and try to be as natural as possible. I say how important the scheme was for me, how much I enjoyed it and that it was thanks to my teachers that I got into it.

Writing about this has reminded me of my first-ever contact with the military, shortly before Dad became seriously ill. Just as I was coming up to my fifteenth birthday, I decided to do something that was totally out of character. I went on a trip with my school to the Army base in Crickhowell for a training course. This came about because all the boys in my senior school class were dead keen to do it and, as I was always seen as the ultimate girlie girl, they kept joking that I would never put my name down. But I did. Apart from me, there was only one other girl who had volunteered, so we were truly outnumbered by a whole load of boys.

Did I live to regret it? Well, the potential to do so was certainly there but, no, I didn't. That doesn't mean the army didn't give me a hard time on the commando assault course, where I'd never seen so much mud in my life. There I was, trying to keep myself together—which, in my case, meant damage limitation, keeping up appearances: trying to protect my hairdo, make-up and not break any nails—all of which clearly drove the instructor doolally.

'You wanna be in the army?' he kept bellowing at me, his face an inch from mine. 'You're too pretty to be in the army.'

At one stage, putting his foot on my back, he pushed me face-down into the mud. Can you believe that? I thought it was *fab-lous*. The truth is that although I played up to everybody, and pretended I was hating every minute, I loved it and thought it all great fun.

I still have video footage of me doing that

course, and I remember Mum and Dad being in hysterics when they watched it.

*   *   *

One reason I am so grateful that I went to Gorseinon College in Swansea to do my A levels in Music, Welsh, History and Dance is that it was there that the principal and her husband, Penny and Les Ryan, suggested that when I finished my A levels I should go to music college. They were the first to suggest this and, needless to say, I got really fired up by this idea.

When I said I hadn't a clue how to go about getting a placc, they were wonderful. They helped me to get application forms for five music colleges: the Royal Northern in Manchester, and the Royal Academy of Music, the Guildhall School of Music and Drama, Trinity College of Music and the Royal College of Music, all in London.

I remember that while I was at Gorseinon College in 1998, singing in the college choir at the Branwyn Hall in Swansea, I had what can only be described as a shattering moment. As the soloist that night in 'O Holy Night', I was being backed by the choir and had just reached the last line 'O night divine, O night . . .', which requires a top B; as my voice soared to reach this there was a sudden, explosive bang. The Branwyn Hall is a recital hall, rather than a theatre, so there are no curtains, just a stage, then the auditorium and, as everybody in the audience gasped, obviously convinced there had been some kind of explosion, I decided to be professional and continue singing—you know, 'the show must go on' and all that. As I finished the

59

carol, I looked up and saw all these fragments of glass falling down from the ceiling showering the people below—and I realised that my top note had shattered the glass panels of one of the lights. Luckily nobody was hurt.

Since then I've been told that these shattering moments have something to do with the frequency of the note and the type of glass that is used, and these two factors have to coincide in order to achieve such a dramatic effect. I must say if I ever have any time on my hands to be mischievous, I would love to repeat that moment. Wouldn't that make a good party trick!

Meanwhile, between these fun and games and studying for my A levels at the college, I got a job working as a waitress two nights a week, then continued to support my studies by getting a part-time job at Safeways, the newest of our local supermarkets. I always thought this was rather bizarre because, when I was at primary school, we'd gone on a trip to the building site and I'd actually laid one of its foundation bricks.

All in all, I worked as a checkout girl at Safeways for two years until I left Wales. The work was actually well paid for somebody of my age and I never found it particularly arduous. There was a wonderful sense of camaraderie among the staff and they were always very understanding about my singing. If I said I had a concert, they would always do their best to accommodate me.

When the letters started to arrive offering me an audition at the various colleges, Mum, ever willing to help once I had made up my mind, offered to take me to each one of them. The first was at the Royal Northern, Manchester. It did not go well.

When I entered the room and went through my paces, singing 'Cara Sposa' by Handel and 'The Watermill' by Vaughan Williams, the songs that my teacher John Huw Thomas had selected for the occasion, one of the people present said, 'You are singing all the wrong songs, young lady. You are not a mezzo-soprano, you are an alto.' 'No,' I protested, flustered. 'I'm definitely a mezzo-soprano.'

Although I was careful to measure my answer and say this very politely, it did not go down well; and, as they all seemed to be in agreement with each other, I was left feeling very wrong-footed—nervous, convinced I wouldn't stand a chance at any of the other auditions that had been lined up because I was singing the wrong songs.

It was not, I must admit, the first time that someone had said they thought I was an alto; and yet others had said I was a soprano. A soprano, of course, is the highest female voice; mezzo-soprano is the middle female voice; and the contralto is the lowest female voice.

The fact that confusion sometimes arises when classifying singers' voices is not really surprising. It takes time for a singer's voice to mature and settle but, in my heart of hearts, I always believed I was a mezzo-soprano—and would remain a mezzo-soprano; and what's more, my singing teacher, John Huw Thomas, was gratifyingly reassuring about me being a mezzo-soprano.

'There are lots of good sopranos out there,' he said, 'but not so many mezzo-sopranos—and even fewer really good mezzo-sopranos.'

I was happy with that but, after my horrible experience at the Royal Northern—where I was also told in the end that they would give me a place if I agreed to wait till next year, when they thought my voice would be more developed—I felt very unsettled. Taking a gap year out was not something I wanted to do. I wanted to go to music college there and then.

I found the whole process of going for auditions petrifying. For these occasions, would-be students had to do a singing audition, followed by a written audition, followed by an oral test, followed by a one-to-one meeting and an interview, so each audition took a whole day; and each ended in the same way: 'Thank you for coming to see us; you will receive a letter.' A variation, I guess, of the notorious 'Don't call us. We'll call you.'

These days I don't suffer from nerves or stage-fright before performances but, back then, because it was very intense and I badly wanted to get into a music college and didn't want to wait another single moment, I was positively shaking with nerves, so very afraid I would fail in my endeavours.

I realise now how lucky I was to have come from the family I did and to have attended the schools I went to, where people were always ready to encourage me and never made me feel like a geek. Sometimes, these days, when I meet students who are the age I was then, I can see they don't get it: don't identify with just how focused, motivated and disciplined I was then; how desperate I was to be with people of my own age, who were on my wavelength, part of my mindset, and who felt as passionately about their music as I did about mine. But that's how it always was for me, and even my boyfriend, Kevin, remained ever-supportive and understood just how driven I was.

After my unfortunate experience at the Royal Northern, the next audition, this time at Trinity College, London, took a turn for the better, and restored some of my self-confidence. I was offered, almost by return of post, a scholarship. Then, while I was still considering this, I went for my audition at the Royal Academy of Music (RAM). There were three people present at this audition and, because I was overawed and terrified, I was convinced I could have done much better. The most important thing when singing is to get the emotion across and, on that occasion, fear had definitely constricted my throat.

After about a week of holding my breath, biting my nails, tossing and turning, and rushing every morning to check the post, the letter came. It was good news: RAM, which I had heard such good things about and was my first choice, had offered me a scholarship. I couldn't have been happier and I couldn't wait to go.

Situated on Marylebone Road in central London, adjacent to one of the capital's most beautiful open spaces, Regent's Park, the RAM is considered to be one of the world's leading music institutions. With students from over fifty countries following diverse programmes that include instrumental performance, conducting, composition, jazz, musical theatre and opera, it promised to be a real seat of learning, not to mention a lot of fun. Among its notable students, I read in its literature, were Lesley Garrett, Dame Felicity Lott and Sir Elton John—and now, I could hardly believe it, I was to follow in their footsteps and be a student there.

SIX

A MIXED BAG

I have to laugh when I look back on the days when I first arrived in London. Country bumpkin that I was, I walked along the streets, beaming away and saying hello to everyone who passed because that's what I was used to doing in Wales. It didn't take me long to realise, though, that this was not the time or the place to say hello. People clearly thought I was an oddball, crazy even, when I did and were giving me a wide berth; and those I greeted on the Tube looked even more uneasy. Such greetings, I soon twigged, were not exchanged in London except by nutters or those who were on drugs or those who knew each other. There was so much to get used to, so much to learn about life in the capital.

In many ways, I realise now, I was a naive eighteen year old, which makes it even more remarkable that Mum was so good about letting me follow my dreams and go. It couldn't have been easy for her to entrust me to the 'big city'. Nevertheless, she swallowed her anxieties, gave me a hand with packing everything into the car, drove me up to London and helped me move into the flat. She even put a coat of paint on all the walls and the woodwork of my room, set everything up and helped me make it cosy and homely, while Kevin installed a new light and set up all my electrical things.

The flat, in Paddington's Little Venice, belonged to Huw Evans, a friend from Neath. His parents had bought it for him when, to their great delight, he'd got a place at Trinity College of Music. As he was the only person I knew in London, I was very relieved when he asked me to be his flatmate.

The flat itself, one of many in what was a very run-down multicultural council block, always smelled of curries, and in all the time I lived there I never saw any of the neighbours. I could walk down the Marylebone Road from there and be in the RAM within half an hour.

I was so lucky to live in this area. Little Venice, a name that was coined apparently by the poet Robert Browning, is an oasis of leafy calm, just minutes from Paddington Station (from where I would take the train home to Wales).

London, though, was a mixed blessing for me when I first arrived. I loved the hustle and bustle, the constant buzz of excitement and energy, but I found it really hard. There I was, living away from Mum and Laura and the rest of the family, and separated from Kevin in a place where nobody wanted to talk to me or laughed at my accent. Where I'd come from, everyone knew everyone else, but in the capital nobody seemed to have time for anybody.

Looking back now, however, I can see that it was this period, when I left home for the first time, which sorted out all the feelings of estrangement I'd been experiencing with Mum after Dad died. Being away from home, I suddenly realised how important Mum was to me, began to appreciate how much she had always done for me and what a lovely comfortable life I had had back home. I wasn't by any means spoiled, but nevertheless I had had everything done for me.

Having taken stock, then, my relationship with Mum became as close as it had been before I became a bolshy teenager and, since then, it's got better and better and we have become really good friends. My mum's a lovely person, very strong yet, at the same time, sensitive—so sensitive that she often avoids discussing delicate issues for fear of upsetting me or anyone else. She's also the life and soul of all our family parties and get-togethers.

I also missed Laura, and felt this especially at night. We had, after all, shared a bedroom until I moved to London and I was so aware when I climbed into bed that she was no longer sleeping above me on the top bunk. Later, of course, she came to stay with me and used to visit me on the London Eye, where I had got a part-time job, working as a tour guide. I might have been Welsh, but I was a quick learner, and there were not many landmarks I hadn't learned to recognise . . . I can still give a pretty good tour of London from the sky!

Despite my initial loneliness in London, I had no regrets and was loving that my life was so adventurous. Apart from myself and Huw, I didn't know anybody else who'd gone to music college. Where we came from the majority of youngsters found local jobs or went to Cardiff University. Only a small percentage travelled as far afield as London.

I was so relieved to turn up at the RAM on the first day of term and find myself in such a *fab-lous* class. There were only eight of us and I was the youngest. I'd been apprehensive that I'd find myself among a bunch of geeks and that everybody would be standoffish and either posh or 'precious'.

I couldn't have been more wrong. My classmates were all so normal and down-to-earth and from day one we were forever having a good laugh together. In no time at all, we all became great friends, and my fears of being lonely dissolved. They really were lovely and I'm still in touch with most of them.

On my first day at the RAM, for example, I met Lucy from Staffordshire and Edda, from Iceland, both sopranos, and the two girls I eventually went on to share a flat with in Paddington; then there was Robert from Jamaica, Cheryl from London, David, a countertenor from Salisbury, another David from Yorkshire and William from South Africa. I loved the fact that while they all obviously shared my passion for singing, they also loved going out, doing fun things and having a good laugh. That made me so happy.

When the day finished at the college, our class would go out together—the capital was our oyster. Always spoiled for choice, we'd get standby tickets for the English National Opera or go to concerts at the Royal Festival Hall, Wigmore Hall, the Barbican, St John's Smith Square, anything that took our fancy. As I was with people who shared my interests, we never lacked for conversation or things to do, and we were all determined to make the most of what London had to offer.

The RAM itself was everything I had hoped for. The emphasis of my course was on classical training—on learning to sing in Italian, French and German and, by the time I left the Academy when I was twenty-two, I had achieved a Bachelor of Music degree in performance. Nobody during my student days ever mentioned commercial recordings, but I always knew that I would want to go into a recording studio some time in the future and make a CD.

In all, I had four years at the Academy and I loved every one of them. It was such a vibrant, energetic place. Each week I had a one-and-a-half hour lesson with my singing teacher, Beatrice Unsworth, and half an hour with Geoffrey Pratley, my vocal coach—the tutor who helps you with your repertoire, the choosing of songs and also with learning the music that you then take to your singing teacher to help you with technique.

In addition there were various song classes to attend that specialised in English song, German lieder, French song and Italian song. I love singing in all these different languages, but fifteen-minute, one-to-one sessions once a week with a language coach never really seemed long enough. Students tended to take their Dictaphone or tape recorders along to these, so they could record the sessions and revise at home. As well as all those classes, we had sight-reading, dance and Alexander Technique classes to help us with our posture and breathing. When it came to getting a degree, it was also necessary to take written and oral tests, and this part of the studies was linked to King's College, London.

Next door to the RAM, there is an annexe with three floors of almost cupboard-size practice rooms, complete with pianos. How much practise we put in was left entirely up to us, but we were expected to use any time that was left over from our structured timetable to practise. Sometimes we were lucky to find a pianist to work with; at other times we had to manage on our own. Come exam times, when everything became very intense, we would almost have to fight for an accompanist, and sometimes we would sit in the corridors for ages, waiting for another student to vacate a room.

When we were in the throes of all this, it was easy to forget there was a world outside the Academy. We lived and breathed the RAM, and when I went to visit some of the friends I had made at other universities, I was surprised, and envious, of their student life, which included a students' bar and a very active union, which was so good at organising events. As it was a relatively small college, all we had was a tiny bar, which was hardly conducive to socialising because only a small number of students at a time could fit into it. I was lucky, though. All the students in my class 'clicked' with each other from day one and, determined it shouldn't be all work and no play, we sorted out our own social life.

To be fair to the Academy, we did occasionally have student parties and always had an end-of-year ball, for which the student union would hire a venue. But, more often than not, we set up our own parties, and, certainly during the first couple of years, we went out to clubs in the West End when they put on student nights, or offered cheap drinks. Money, of course, was always in short supply, but Mum helped me a lot by paying my rent for the entire time I was at the Academy. Despite this, I still ended up taking out a student loan and left the RAM with a horrendous debt that hung heavily around my neck.

Thanks to my Mum and Dad, though, I had very good money sense and knew how to pace myself. They were such good role models. If they wanted something for the house, such as a new washing

69

machine, they would shop around for the very best deal, save until they had the money, and even then agonise about whether or not they should do it. Only then, decision made, would they go out and buy it—and that kind of sensible approach has remained with me.

All in all, during my days at the RAM, I still managed to do all the things that students do and I came out knowing what I would like to repeat and what I wouldn't. By the time I left, I'd done the teenage thing, the all-night partying, knew what it was like to have had too much to drink and feel like a bear with a sore head the next day. But I'm glad about all that. These days, still in my twenties, I don't feel I'm missing out on anything, and I don't really go clubbing any more. In fact, my idea of a perfect evening in London is relaxing with friends over dinner, then when I'm back home in Neath, going out to the pub to have a drink with my old schoolmates. Alcohol, sadly, is off limits most of the time for singers as it dehydrates the throat.

In some respects, throughout all my years at the RAM, I did find London an unsafe and frightening place. Like any capital city, I was only too aware that it had its dangers and problems, its fair share of drunks, addicts, muggers and loonies wandering around, and, as it happened, I was not to be spared from experiencing the darker side of London life, an experience that could so easily have cost me my life.

By the time this terrifying event occurred, I had been in London for a couple of years and had become great friends with two students in my class, Edda and Lucy, who were now sharing the flat in Paddington with me—the flat that belonged to

Huw, who had recently returned to Wales.

On that awful night, which so nearly ended in disaster for me, we had been out celebrating William's birthday at Brown's restaurant in Covent Garden. Usually on occasions such as these, which we knew would end rather late, Lucy, Edda and I always made sure we would travel home together; and still, for the life of me, I cannot work out how we became separated after we left the restaurant that night. But we did. I only know that one moment the three of us were together, having a great time chatting away as we crossed Leicester Square, and the next I was alone with the two boys called David from my class, who had also been part of William's birthday celebrations.

I wasn't too worried at first, just continued to keep a lookout for the girls as I walked towards Piccadilly to get the bus back to Paddington. But when the boys and I reached the bus stop and there was still no sign of Edda and Lucy, we had to go our separate ways because they lived in Bermondsey.

The bus journey itself was uneventful, just a few rowdy lads on the top deck having fun. All was well, in fact, until I got off the bus by Paddington Station. Normally this is a busy area, with plenty of pedestrians crossing Bishop's Bridge Road, a route I had to take to get to the flat, which was just two minutes away on the other side. But it was deserted that night.

Realising I would need to go through the narrow pedestrian tunnel, just the other side of the bridge, I decided, as a precaution, to call my flatmates on my mobile to tell them that I was on the bridge and that I'd be home in two minutes. Just as I got through to Lucy, though, and was telling her where I was, I sensed a presence behind me. A tall man, dressed in respectable, casual city clothes, was standing, too close for comfort, right by my left shoulder. I knew at once that, despite his respectable appearance, he was up to no good.

'Lucy,' I gasped, 'there's a man . . .'

I didn't have time to finish the sentence. A split second later, without saying a word, he just leaped around to the front of me, grabbed me by my left arm and began dragging me down a gangway that led to a pitch-black, single-lane driveway that had once been used by cars that were about to be loaded on to a train at the station. I was absolutely terrified.

My first thought, as he grunted and dragged me along, was that he was going to murder me; my second was that he was going to rape me. I was still clutching my mobile phone in my right hand, and still connected to my flatmates, who could hear my screams and everything that was going on. I made one desperate attempt to offer him my mobile phone and my wallet, which I was clutching in my left hand, but I knew by then that this was not a mugging, not a robbery. If it were, he could easily have snatched my mobile and wallet and been on his way by now. His intention was to rape me.

It was lucky for me that this attempted assault occurred at a time when I was going to the gym a great deal and I was, therefore, very fit. Somehow, I managed to pull back from him, slip my hand from his grasp and, once free from his clutches, sprinted to the other side of the bridge—a bridge that was normally so busy with traffic, but now, when I needed it most, deserted.

Having reached the other side of the pavement, where there was a huge wooden fence, I continued to run alongside this in my five-inch high heels. How I managed to get as far as I did, I will never know, but my few moments of freedom were about to come to a violent end.

Just as I thought I might make it to the other end of the bridge, he suddenly loomed alongside me again and punched me with such force that I ricocheted off the wooden fence and hit the ground.

Until this kind of thing happens, you do not know how you will react; you have no idea whether you will freeze or put up a fight. What I knew instinctively, though, is that if I could curl up into a small tight ball, he would not be able to rape me. He could kick me, which he did over and over again, but he could not rape me. So that is what I did.

I didn't try to get up; I just lay on the ground in a small tight ball and endured him kicking me in a fruitless attempt to open me up. After a while, I sensed that he was tiring and had realised that he was not going to get anywhere. So, raising my head a fraction, I murmured: 'What do you want?'

'Oh, just give me your purse, then,' he snapped back.

Realising the worst was over, I reached up and handed him my diamanté-encrusted purse, which he snatched out of my hand before running off. As he reached the other end of the bridge, though, he suddenly stopped and, for one heart-stoppingly awful moment, I thought he was coming back to try again. But, no, this time, he just stood there looking back at me, then laughing aloud as if it had all been a game, he calmly walked off towards the station.

Precisely at that moment, just as he was disappearing out of sight, my two flatmates came running towards me in their pyjamas. Having heard the entire attack on the phone, they were absolutely frantic, convinced I would be dead or raped by the time they reached me. Then, a few minutes later, the police, whom the girls had had the presence of mind to call, arrived in their squad car.

A little later when I was giving my statement to the officers, I kept emphasising that I would remember my attacker's face for as long as I lived—and I meant it. I would still recognise him today. As I had put up quite a struggle when he was dragging me towards the drive-in, I'd had plenty of time to take in his appearance. I also kept repeating that what had scared me more than anything was how respectable he looked. A white man, aged between thirty and thirty-five, about six feet tall, and clean-cut, he smelled as if he had just come out of a pub where he had been for a drink after a day at the office.

We were all still so shocked and petrified after the police left that Lucy and I had to sleep in the same bed; and, although I spoke to a victim-support counsellor on the phone, it was months before I stopped feeling threatened by some unseen danger at night.

What bothered me later about the police investigation into the attack on me was that, although the officers were obviously doing their best, when it came to showing me mugshots and photo-fits, there were only three or four mugshots of white men. The rest, by far the majority, were black; and there were certainly no shots of a man who was respectably dressed in city-slicker clothes and shoes.

What was also scary was that, although I had cancelled my credit card, the attacker kept using it in pubs around the Paddington area, so it was obvious he either worked or lived locally, something that supported the police theory that it was an opportunistic attack, that he was on the same bus as me that night and looking for someone to follow.

That attack left me with several legacies. To this day, I hate walking anywhere after dark on my own, even if it is just a short distance; and I have become very protective of my sister, Laura. Ever since then, whenever Laura comes to meet me for dinner, I insist on giving her the money for a taxi home. There is no way, as far as I'm concerned, that she is going home on the Tube and walking across Clapham Common in the dark.

One day recently I went past the flats where I used to live with Edda and Lucy and noticed that now the building work in the area has been completed and Bishops Bridge Road re-opened, the driveway where I was attacked no longer exists.

There is a postscript to this horrible story. Two years after the attack, I was watching an episode of *Crimewatch*, which was dealing with the case of a girl who had been raped underneath one of London's bridges, and the description she gave of the man convinced me that her attacker was the same man who had attacked me. I thought about calling in that night, but then I wondered what it would achieve? I had already told the police everything I knew.

The attack didn't affect my attitude to men because all the men in my life have always been so gentle and kind, and each one who heard about the attack took the stance of 'Oh, my God! I'll kill him if I ever get the chance.'

What has protected me from long-term psychological damage is the belief that even horrible events like that can make you stronger. I believe that all the mistakes I have made in my life have taught me the most important lessons; and I have discovered things about myself, and resources within myself, that I didn't know were there.

Laura loved coming to London to stay with me, but she was also very shaken by my being attacked. Fortunately, this didn't put her off moving to London a bit later. By then she had had some hairy situations herself when travelling around south Asia and her attitude, like mine, was that you can't let such things stop you.

After that attack, I managed to scrape enough money together from my London Eye job to buy an old banger.

I loved working on the Eye—and I've just remembered that one day while I was assisting at the weekend in Customer Services, we received a letter from the Islington Society for the Blind saying that a group of their members would like to book a trip on the Eye. Initially, everybody in the office looked rather incredulous and kept saying: 'But what's the point of blind people going on the Eye?' I instinctively felt, however, that I understood and I said: 'I'll do it—I'll take them up.'

On the day, having greeted them and got them

all on board the pod, I began the event by saying: 'I know it's going to be difficult for some of you, so I'm going to be your eyes and tell you what I can see. Okay?'

Everything went really well and just as we finished the ascent and were coming down the other side, one man said: 'How come somebody with such a lovely Welsh accent is working in London?' Then when I told them I was studying singing at the Royal Academy of Music, they asked me if I would sing for them, so, as this was obviously an audio rather than a visual outing for them, I said: 'Okay' and sang some Mozart for them on the way down. The acoustics were really good in the pod, and they were all such lovely appreciative listeners.

There is a lovely postscript to this story. After I'd got my record deal and was on my first live tour, a letter came to my dressing-room from the Islington Society for the Blind, saying: 'Ever since that day on the Eye, we always knew you were going to be a star. We've followed your career, bought your album and tonight we will be in the front row.' I was so touched I shared this experience with the rest of the audience by reading their letter out on stage.

*   *   *

By the time I went to the Royal Academy of Music, Kevin and I had been together for nearly four years and, throughout my early days there, I used to go home to Wales every weekend on the train to see him and also to perform as a soloist in concerts, choirs and weddings. During that time, although I was only 5ft 5in, too small for catwalk work, I was also doing some modelling. Later, in the year 2000, my mum entered me in a modelling competition, which I won and was named the Face of Wales 2000.

I was never tempted, though, to change course and make modelling my career. It was just another way of topping up funds and I had my heart set on other things. That was just as well because I wasn't really thin or tall enough for a full-time modelling job. Also, modelling seemed to be all about not eating or taking on faddy diets in order to look good, whereas singing is all about 'your body is your instrument' and the need to eat well to be healthy. The two careers don't really mix. I'd always been a curvaceous girl who loved glamour—and adored Marilyn Monroe—and my brief period in modelling didn't change any of that.

We had no lessons on a Friday and so every Thursday night during my first year at the RAM, I tackled the three-hour train journey from Paddington to Neath, then returned again on Sunday night. Kevin paid for my train fares or I wouldn't have been able to do it. The constant travelling to and fro was exhausting though; and worse, by far, was that we were now living such different lives, we were growing apart. In the end, just after the Millennium arrived to all that fanfare and razzmatazz, I faced up to telling Kevin that I thought we had grown apart and should go our separate ways. I knew this was right but I found it devastating.

I couldn't have wished for a more perfect boyfriend. He was such a lovely guy, an absolute gentleman who taught me what a loving relationship should be like; and, to this day, my relationship with him remains my benchmark. Thanks to Kevin, I know just how beautiful being in love can be, and I realise how lucky I was. I am only too aware of just how fortunate I was that Kevin was such a perfect first love. I'm still in touch with him, and he now has a girlfriend whom I am sure he will marry.

I honestly don't think any of us can truly understand love until we have experienced the anguish of loss. That terrible feeling that churns in your stomach is indescribable. Yes, I had decided that we had to call it off, but that didn't make it any easier. I still missed him.

SEVEN

SOME ENCHANTED EVENING . . .

When it comes to relationships, I am a true believer in the 'Some enchanted evening, you will see a stranger across a crowded room' syndrome. I really am a romantic when it comes to love and matters of the heart—and what I mean by that is that it's the one time I am impulsive and therefore tend to get swept off my feet.

And that's how it was, when a year after being single and going out only with the friends I'd made at the Royal Academy of Music, I met Steve Hart, who, within seconds, had found the short cut to my heart.

The occasion was a party at a nightclub. I was standing at the bar, chatting to my cousin, Melanie, who had replaced Edda in the flat when Edda moved in with her boyfriend, when in walked Steve. As I glanced up, it was as if he was lit by a spotlight. 'Oh, my God, Mel!' I said. He really was the most *gorg-eous* man I had ever set eyes upon and I'm quite sure I fell in love with him there and then. This was on 27 February 2001, just three months before my twenty-first birthday; and after spending that evening chatting with Steve, we started dating.

Steve, I discovered was in the music business: he had been chosen by Simon Cowell of American TV's *American Idol* to be a member of the boy band Worlds Apart, and had signed a record deal with Sony BMG.

Like most girls I like to be romanced and guys

80

with good manners are few and far between. But Steve was a total gentleman from the beginning and always treated me like a lady. We had a lot in common and loved creating memories to tuck them into a memory bank—things that make you smile when you look back on them. Later, when we were so often apart, we both loved saying: 'D'you remember when we . . . ?' It always brought us closer together, warmed our hearts and made us laugh. Good memories are like treasured snapshots, which you can get out and share whenever you are in the mood or whenever the need arises.

For my twenty-first birthday, Steve gave me a lovely silver Rolex watch and for my twenty-second birthday, Steve booked us a surprise trip to Florida. I was thrilled. I'd never been to America and the thought of having such an incredible adventure together was so romantic. As Steve had hired a car, a convertible, we were able to explore the whole coast of Florida, stopping in motels along the way; we felt like the characters in a movie. We travelled around like this for three glorious, carefree weeks, then when we reached Fort Lauderdale we took a boat to the Bahamas where we stayed for the last couple of days.

By the time we returned, we had lived through one enchanted evening after another and were so in love we couldn't bear to be apart—so I said a fond farewell to my flatmates, Lucy and Edda, and moved in with Steve. We could not have been happier. Bliss.

*   *   *

81

So all was well in my love life, and all was well at the Academy where I continued to work hard with Beatrice, my singing teacher, and at my other studies. But there was a shadow dogging my footsteps during my twenty-first year. Somewhere along the line, I don't quite know when, I had ceased to be happy with my curvaceous body; I had started to criticise how I looked and had developed quite a serious eating disorder.

I had avoided anorexia and bulimia during my teenage years, but now I was convinced I was overweight and fat, and felt matters would only get worse if I didn't keep to a very strict diet and work out at a gym at least twice a day, every day. I'd always had a tendency to be a perfectionist, somebody who has to be totally in control of everything, and now I had also become obsessional and was checking and rechecking every morsel I ate. During this time I would eat only salad stuff, plus one Weetabix—and that was it for the day. Part of me knew I was being unreasonable and much too faddy, but I couldn't help myself.

Things began to get really serious after I began the Atkins Diet, a diet that everybody, including a number of celebrities, was raving about at that time. For this diet you are supposed to go for two weeks eating only protein, then slowly re-introduce carbohydrates. But, true to the control freak that I was, I became hooked on the protein-only part of the diet and never brought back the carbohydrates. For eight months I continued to eat proteins only, while working out obsessively in the gym, and in no time at all my weight had dropped to under seven stones. By this time, I didn't feel at all well and my bodily functions were not functioning as they should've been; but, although I am sure I looked horrendous, people kept telling me I looked great, which encouraged me to continue.

Steve, however, was getting really rattled and was not so complimentary: 'You're all skin and bones,' he kept warning me, 'you're not looking anywhere near as good as you used to when you were a gorgeous, curvy woman.' That stopped me in my tracks for a moment or two, but when I looked in the mirror I could still see excess fat on me and was convinced I still had lots of weight to lose. By then, I was truly in the grip of an eating disorder, and I even began to enjoy people saying: 'Katherine, you are *too* thin . . .'

Steve was worried, Mum was worried, but as far as I was concerned they had become the enemy. In my confused state of mind, I thought they were trying to spoil my fun and didn't want me to look good. It was not until I got some photographs back after Steve and I had been on holiday that I was shocked into seeing what I was doing to myself. There, in all the pictures, was somebody I didn't recognise, somebody with a huge head on top of tiny shoulders and a stick-insect body. I was aghast. Was that really me? Was that what I looked like? It was a wake-up call; but as by then I didn't know how to start eating properly again, I could only carry on as before.

I dread to think what would have happened if Mum had not come to stay with me at that time. When we went out for dinner that night, having noticed how picky I was being about food and how little I had ordered for my main course, she said in a voice that invited no argument, 'You obviously need some sugar.' As the sweet trolley went past, she ordered an enormous piece of chocolate mudcake. I was petrified.

'I'll be as sick as a dog,' I protested.

'Good, but it will break the cycle and set you back on the right track,' Mum replied.

By then as I was already aware of the harm I was doing myself and the guilt was setting in, but I did what Mum said and ate as much of the cake as I could manage without disgracing myself at the table. For twenty-four hours after that I was violently sick and could hardly leave the bathroom, but during that horrendous time, I began to accept that I had taken the Atkins diet to extremes, and that my self-imposed excesses were making me feel woozy all day and unable to sleep at night.

After that, I listened to Mum and Steve and knew I had to do something to get me out of what had become a potentially life-threatening nose-dive. I started, slowly but surely, to include a few spoonfuls of fruit and vegetables in my diet, and then began to eat slices of toast. Even so, it was ages before the scales began to register any return of the weight I had lost.

Since then, I have once again settled into being myself and feeling comfortable in my own skin. I am no longer obsessed with changing my body image, but just accept myself as I am. At the moment I am a pesco-vegetarian, who veers on the side of being vegan when I am at home, which means I don't eat any dairy products either. But at least I have fresh fruit and vegetables, nuts and seeds on a daily basis; and, as I now do everything in moderation, if I really fancy something I have it. As for the dairy products, they are inclined to cause catarrh and are not good for the voice anyway.

These days, I want to warn young girls, and boys for that matter, not to believe all the mega slimline images they see in glossy magazines. Through my work, I have come to realise that most of these images have been airbrushed or digitally enhanced. I've seen so many pictures of myself that have been given this kind of treatment in art departments, and I'm happy to tell anybody who's willing to listen that I don't really look as perfect as I appear in some pictures. There is far too much pressure on us looking great and skinny all the time. Wouldn't it be great if the emphasis could move to the kind of people we are within?

*   *   *

During my last year at the Academy, Steve said he would come to a recital that I was giving there and that a friend of ours, Steve DuBerry, a songwriter/producer who had produced two of Tina Turner's number one hits, was also going to come along. Steve DuBerry, by the way, had also been nominated for a Grammy, a highly sought after award that is presented annually by the National Academy of Recording Arts for outstanding achievements in the record business. The Grammys are, in fact, considered to be the US record industry's equivalent of the Oscars.

There was nothing particularly special about the recital I was giving that night, but the evening itself turned out to be a really special evening that was destined to change my life. I had often mentioned to Steve DuBerry that it was my ambition to make a CD of my own one day and, when we all went out together after the recital, he suddenly said:

'Katherine, why don't you make that demo tape?'

'I'd really love to do,' I replied. 'That would be *fab-lous*.'

'Then let's do it,' he said.

'I'm not sure I'd know how to go about it,' I answered.

'But *I* do,' Steve said.

And, looking at him, I realised he was serious; he was actually offering to help me. He was such a successful, busy guy, I could hardly believe my luck—but I immediately said: 'Okay, Steve, let's do it.'

'What do you make of Steve's offer?' I asked my Steve on the way home that night.

'I think it's great,' he replied. 'Steve really knows his stuff and he clearly thinks you are the talented person we know you are.'

I was so excited at the thought of going to a studio to work with Steve to make a demo, I didn't sleep a wink that night.

*   *   *

By the day of the recording, I'd chosen two pieces to sing. One was Pergolesi's 'Stabat Mater', the other was Delibes's 'Flower Duet' from *Lakmé*, which Steve arranged over a dance beat. We also did two pop-songs, written by Steve himself. One of these was a ballad, the other a Nina Simone type of song.

Just being in a recording studio was exciting in itself. There was so much I needed to learn about how studios work when you are doing different 'takes' and the various effects that can be created to bring it all together. But Steve was a brilliant

86

teacher, very together and patient, and so good at answering all my questions.

We did lots of takes that day, primarily because I had to get used to singing with a microphone, which requires a completely different technique to that of projecting your voice in a concert hall. As in acting, less of everything is often better, so deliberate minimalism, I learned, is the order of the day.

Having done the demo, I carried on at the Academy but, unbeknown to me, Steve had passed the demo to his management team, who set about passing it around various record companies. Meanwhile, although everyone else in my year at the RAM had decided to stay on to do a postgraduate course, I decided to put my teacher's diploma, which I had taken in my fourth year, to good use.

The plan I had in mind was to take two years out and earn some money from teaching, so that I could then return and do the postgraduate course and hopefully gain a Master's degree. In the meantime, I also made arrangements to continue my singing lessons with Beatrice, my teacher at the Academy.

Later I became one of the youngest people ever to be made an associate of the Royal Academy of Music in London, a very special honour that is conferred on 'distinguished former students'.

My first job when I left the RAM was a Saturday job teaching at a stage school called Future Faces in Enfield, Middlesex. I had three classes of five-to-eights, eight-to-twelves and thirteen-pluses. I absolutely loved them all and I adored teaching. It was so refreshing. I'd been in such a pressurised, intense atmosphere for so long, in a situation where everyone around me was also stressed, that it was really nice to be among children, especially the young ones, who were so excited and thrilled just to be singing. It reminded me that that was why I had wanted to sing myself, why I loved singing. The teaching of others, in fact, rekindled my own passion, re-energised me. I also loved the fact that I was close to some of the older students in age—I was twenty-two and many of them were eighteen.

As well as the stage school, I was offered a job at St Mary's High School, Cheshunt, Hertfordshire, as a peripatetic teacher, going in two days a week for fifteen- to thirty-minute sessions. These were extra lessons, paid for by parents, for children who wanted to sing or who were doing GCSE music. As I now had about thirty different kinds of students in all, my teaching was now a three-day-a-week job.

The sessions at St Mary's were always one-to-ones and I started by doing the things they wanted to do, such as pop songs or musical theatre, before starting on the singing exams. At the stage schools, though, it was mostly pop songs and music theatre that were required, and at the end of every year the stage school put on a show. This was all very reminiscent of my time in *Calamity Jane*, and getting the whole class or the whole school involved was tremendous fun. One song I particularly remember from that period was 'Sit Down You're Rocking the Boat' from the show *Guys and Dolls*. It was so amazing watching the children enjoy performing, like I had.

I also took on teaching jobs at Heathcote School and Barnwell School, both in Stevenage, Hertfordshire, and two evening classes at the

My parents'
wedding day.

In Mum's arms, around two
months old, outside
Aunty Louise's.

Me at about
five months.

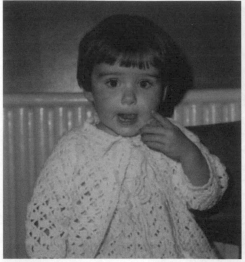

Left Me at twenty months. *Right* I've always loved dressing up. Here I am as a buzzy bee in a mother and toddler group party, Christmas 1983.

I laughed for a good twenty minutes when I found this photo. This is me and Laura (who was always my little friend) in the bath in Wellfield Avenue, 1983.

Me, Mum and Laura up the Gnoll, the country park near where we lived in 1984.

The family home in Neath.

Left Two little Welsh girls on St David's Day outside my primary school. I'm holding my Welsh doll, called Bronwyn. *Right* The christingle service after the school play at Alderman Davies. I think I was a shepherd.

Dressing up again!   On holiday in Alcudia in 1986.

Laura and I in the back   Dancing in our new bear slippers.
garden of Wellfield
Avenue (you can see
St David's Church in the background). It's really
hard to find a picture of me where I'm not posing!

For some reason I haven't got many pictures of me and Dad on our own so that's why I love this one. I just wish his eyes were open.

Dad with his favourite munchies, Fruit & Nut!

Dressed up as cats for Halloween.

Tea at Nanna's with Laura, and Melanie and Gavin, my cousins.

Left Me and Laura in our school uniforms. *Right* Mum's favourite school photo (in my summer school uniform).

Mum took this picture of Laura and me on the beach.

Choirgirl of the year competition, 1990. This is my first year, when I came second. I'm the one in the terrible blue hairband.

05/25/99

Kevin. (The inset is a photo of my Royal Academy friends.)

Welsh Choirgirl of the Year 1992. This is the one I won.

With Don McLean after the BBC Radio 2 Choirgirl of the Year final.

With Mum and Laura in 1997.

Graduating from the Royal Academy of Music.

At Nordoff Robbins Music Therapy Carol Service, St Luke's Church, Chelsea in December 2003. (Richard Young/Rex Features)

In my rugby shirt just before I sang as Welsh mascot for the first time, 2003.

My favourite place to sing – at the Millennium Stadium with the Welsh team.

Charlotte Church, Max Boyce and me sing the Welsh national anthem before the 6 Nations Wales v Ireland game in March 2005. (PA Photos)

Left Singing at the Tsunami Relief Concert at the
Millennium Stadium in Cardiff in January 2005 (PA Photos).
Right My mum took this picture of me at my first Classical
BRITs in 2005, where I won the award for best album.

Left Singing at the Brits 2005 (PA Photos) and with Mum at
the party afterwards (Richard Young/Rex Features).

At Port Lympne Wild Animal Park, Kent, feeding three-year-old Asian elephant Sittang in August 2005. (David Hartley/Rex Features)

Performing at the Nobel Peace Prize ceremony in Oslo in 2005. (Corbis)

Taylor Dance School as well as a few private one-to-ones. This meant I was now doing six days a week, so my teaching business had really taken off and I was earning a good sum of money towards my postgraduate studies.

Fate, however, chose this moment to intervene and the children lost the person they insisted on calling 'Miss' to a totally unexpected kind of fame and fortune.

*   *   *

Three months into my teaching career I got a call, completely out of the blue, to say that the demo I had made while I was at the Royal Academy of Music had found its way into the hands of Universal Classics and they wanted me to come to their London offices for a meeting. It took a while for the meaning of the call to sink in; I was beside myself with excitement. I decided to dress smart but casual: jeans and a glamorous jumper, I think. I spent quite a lot of time getting my hair and make-up just right and I had checked online to find out which artists recorded on the Universal label.

I was obviously very nervous on the day but, strangely, when I was called into the actual meeting with Dickon Stainer and Mark Wilkinson at Universal Classics, I was calm. During the meeting they asked me lots of questions about myself and my background and I got the impression that they were looking for somebody who would tick all the boxes they had in mind—but somebody who, at the same time, had their own personality.

As they knew I was Welsh, they asked me if I had done any Eisteddfods—the largest festival of competitive music and poetry in Europe. The youth Eisteddfod, which is organised by Wales's largest youth movement, Urdd Gobaith Cymru, brings together children from the age of seven upwards from all across Wales for a week of singing, recitation, dancing, acting and musicianship in the summer half-term school holiday. When I answered 'Yes' to that question, it was obvious to me that this was the response they'd hoped to hear, and they then asked me what I was doing now.

'I'm a teacher,' I replied and, as they looked at each other, I realised I had said something that had ticked another of their boxes. It was almost as if they were saying 'Oh, yes, a teacher, that's good news. We *love* that.' Later on, when I'd wised up a bit, I realised that this meeting was all about marketing, something record companies obviously do have to keep in mind.

*   *   *

For the live showcase with Universal Classics, I decided to do the programme I'd done for my final recital at the RAM: 'Sta nell'ircana' from Alcina; 'Vado ma dove? O Dei!' by Mozart; Mahler's 'Fruhlingsmorgen' and 'Erinnerung'; 'Mandoline' and 'En Sourdine' by Fauré; 'Head, Rain, Storm' from the three Venetian settings and 'Una Voce poco fa' by Rossini.

Universal Classics hired a big studio and as they told me to bring along a pianist I asked Bethany Phillips, a pianist from RAM, to come with me as my accompanist.

On the day, the actual event turned out to be

one of the most daunting and scary experiences of my life, an experience that, these days, enables me to fully understand and sympathise with how the contestants must feel on *The X Factor.* My audition, if I can call it that, was in a huge room and, sitting in front of me at a large table, were three record company executives, Mark and Dickon from the first meeting, plus, this time, Bill Holland and Niki Sanderson, a TV plugger, who organises personal appearances on television and is now my TV plugger. All four of them were poker-faced, the deadpan expressions on their faces obviously designed not to give anything away.

I was already nervous, only too aware that this was a one-off opportunity for me, and the way they were looking at me only made matters worse. The singing went without a hitch and, as the last note faded, I heard Dickon Stainer ask Niki, the TV-plugger, if she thought I was TV material; if she thought from what she'd seen and heard she would be able to get me on TV.

'Oh, yes, no problem,' was Niki's emphatic and gratifying reply. (I love you for saying that, Niki!)

Then they all said, 'Thank you, Katherine,' and I signalled to Bethany, who was still at the piano, that it was time to leave. Just at that moment, Bill Holland said: 'Hold on a minute, Katherine. Do you do musical theatre songs as well as classical?' Now Bethany is a classical pianist and I am a classically trained singer, and even though I had done some musical shows at school and had recently been teaching musical theatre, my mind went blank before shooting into overdrive.

'Yes—yes I do,' I replied, still sounding very dubious.

'Great. Can you sing us something? Anything,' Bill Holland replied.

But what, I was thinking, now completely thrown. Then, hoping that none of this confusion was registering on my face, I turned to Bethany and whispered, 'Do you know "I Dreamed A Dream" from *Les Misérables*?' This was the only musical-theatre song I remembered and knew by heart.

'Yes, I think so,' she whispered back.

Then, both somewhat flummoxed, we busked it. Immediately I stopped singing, I planted a huge grin on my face and said, sounding much more confident than I felt: 'Of course, we've never rehearsed that song together; we've never tried to do it until now.'

'No problem,' Bill Holland replied.

Then everybody got up again, said thank you once more, and Bethany and I left.

'Oh, God,' I was muttering to myself. 'Oh, God.' They had all looked so bored. None of them had showed any real interest, and nothing seemed to register with them. Despite my determination to sing my heart out, I had obviously messed up, ruined my now-or-never chance of a lifetime, blown it.

I was so keen to succeed, I had even taken the time and trouble to prepare an extensive CV, with a photograph attached that had been taken especially by Steve. I really wanted them to go away and think very seriously about taking me on. As I drove home, their 'Thanks, we'll let you know' kept ringing in my ears and, overwrought from all the stress and tension of the day, I started to cry. 'They weren't happy,' I kept telling myself. At one point on that hour's journey back to Steve and the flat, I stopped and called my mum on my mobile.

'I'm sure you did your best, love,' she kept saying to console me. 'That's all we can ever do, Katherine. Try not to be too upset.'

But I was inconsolable. When I walked into the flat, I discovered Steve was ill in bed with a very heavy cold.

'How did it go?' he croaked, trying to rally.

'It was awful,' I replied, always dramatic. 'I didn't get it.'

'You can't be sure of that.'

'I'm sure,' I answered back.

Hardly able to see through my tears of disappointment, I wandered off into the kitchen to make him a hot drink. There were, I discovered, no lemons, which Mum always swore by when one of us had a cold, but I was far too devastated to care about that.

EIGHT

MOMENTOUS MOMENTS

Just one hour after I told Steve I had blown it, my mobile rang. Thinking it was Mum ringing to commiserate with me further, I answered it. It was Universal.

'Yes?' I said, my voice hoarse from crying.

'Katherine,' the voice said, 'we are going to offer you a record deal.'

'No way!' I said, very nearly bursting into tears again. I don't remember much of the conversation after that.

'What's going on?' Steve asked, appearing in the doorway as the call finished.

'I've got a record deal. A record deal, Steve.'

'You're kidding,' he gasped.

'No, it's for real,' I said, bursting into tears.

I had made such a good job of convincing him that I'd failed, he was having difficulty readjusting his thoughts. When it had sunk in, he gave me the kind of hug that you remember for a lifetime. Moments later I called Mum to tell her and burst into tears again. In fact, I spent the whole afternoon bursting into tears. I'd been so certain I'd messed up that half of me still didn't quite believe it—and, when I look back now, I think those guys at Universal were so mean to put me through that. They obviously knew when I was in the studio with them that they were going to offer me a deal, but they remained deadpan.

When I'd got my head together and calmed

106

down a little, I phoned Mum again.

'I don't want anyone but you, Laura and Steve to know I've got a deal,' I said urgently. 'I'm really scared that if I tell anybody else, it won't happen. It's all too good to be true, Mum, and I'm so frightened it will slip through my fingers.'

Even now as I recall the events of that day, it still seems like a fairytale. I had dreamed of something like it happening and had indulged in frequent fantasies about it, but I had never really expected it to happen. I had thought I would go on teaching for a bit, return to the RAM to take my postgraduate degree course, then, with luck, pursue a career in opera, hopefully starting in the chorus of an operatic company and then slowly work my way up to becoming a soloist. But I'd expected all that to be a longish process that would require patience and perseverance.

But now it had happened for me big time, and in record time, while I was still just twenty-two years old. That surely was the 'stuff that dreams are made of'.

*   *   *

We all experience 'firsts' that make up the milestones of our childhood, youth and adult life: the first time we go to school, our first date and goodnight kiss, our first job, and so on, but I never knew so many firsts existed until I was offered my first record deal. There was, for example, the first time I came across people who worked in marketing, publicity and press departments, who explained so much in so little time that my head was left spinning; and then, having got the deal,

Steve advised me to get a business manager; oh, yes, and a contract lawyer and an accountant, as soon as possible. The first time he said this, I replied: 'How do I go about choosing all those, Steve?'

'I'll help you,' he answered.

So he drew up a list of professional managers for us to go and see, but having made appointments to meet several of these, none seemed quite right for me. Then one day, when I was recording my first album at Rive Droit Studio in Kingston, a guy called 'Sir' Harry who ran the studio advised me to think globally. In other words, he was saying I shouldn't choose a manager just based on their success in the UK, but on their achievements around the world. He was the first person, apart from Steve, who had said that to me and, as this was really good advice, I decided to act on the names that he mentioned. One of these was Brian Lane of Bandana Management.

When I walked into Brian's office, which is above a deli in Golborne Road, just off the Portobello Road in Notting Hill, the first thing I noticed was that the walls were crammed with gold and platinum discs; but, as these were all for rock artists such as Yes, Rick Wakeman, Asia, Buggles, a-ha, A-Teens and Vangelis, I really thought for a moment that I was in the wrong place. When I sat down, though, and the meeting began, I realised Brian had a passion for the music business that I hadn't come across before. He was also older than the others I had seen, had been there, got the T-shirt and was obviously very knowledgeable and successful.

It soon became apparent that he was also

enthusiastic about me, not because of the money he thought he could make, but because my kind of music was new to him, something he had not dealt in before, and he kept saying, 'There's nobody like you, Katherine—you're a one-off, the first female in the business who is not copying anybody else.' And as all the artists he had managed up to then had also been one-offs, he was immediately interested. In fact, I remember him saying: 'I like one-offs. After all, who would want a second drip-paint-artist after Jackson Pollock? Originality is everything. Let other people copy you, not the other way round.'

When we knew each other better, Brian reminded me that the first time I came to see him in his office, it was a gloriously hot summer's day and, as I was appropriately dressed for it in a short skirt, his first thought, he told me, was that I did not look like an opera singer; and, to begin with, he just couldn't marry how I actually looked and how I sounded on the disc. Short skirts and 'Ave Maria' do not go together! 'But Katherine,' he thought, 'could be the first of a kind, the most glamorous opera singer in the world.'

'I don't know anything about classical music,' he said during our first meeting, 'but I think you should remain true to yourself and not try to be anything other than what you are.' This, needless to say, was music to my ears.

He then mentioned that he had a good friend in Oslo called Oddarvid Stromstad, who was the producer of the Nobel Peace Prize show, a hugely successful TV show, which is shown every December in Oslo shortly after the Nobel Peace Prize award has been awarded, and then

109

transmitted globally.

'The production team always has a top classical artist on the programme,' he told me. 'How would you feel about going to Oslo with my assistant tomorrow to have lunch with Oddarvid Stromstad?'

Having taken a moment or so to recover my composure, I replied, 'Yes, okay, thank you.' And, later that day, Brian phoned Oddarvid and persuaded him to have lunch with me.

As it happened, I didn't do the Nobel Peace Prize show that year, but I did the following year. And, in between, Brian became my manager. I'm so glad he did. Since those days, I've heard him say on a number of occasions, 'I've managed a lot of successful artists, but Katherine's career is the one that has given me, and still gives me, the most satisfaction. For me, it was a new genre, and, like Katherine, I enjoy a challenge.'

'Artists,' he is fond of saying, 'work incredibly hard and, as their fame increases their privacy decreases. So, there has to be some compensations, some perks on offer—a new target to aim at every year.'

One way or another, I found the kind of energy Brian had, and generated to others, very exciting; and, as I also liked and admired his old-school attitudes and way of doing things, I decided to join forces with him. Since then, what I've really come to love about him is that although everyone thinks he is a hardball player and he likes everyone to think he's tough—and can be when he needs to be—he also has a very kind, gentle side to him.

Other current members of my team are Tara Joseph, an absolute gem, who joined me in 2007. She's my personal manager, who works with me on

110

a daily basis, manages my schedule and also travels with me; Barrie Evans, who is my stage manager on tour, Sharon Wilmore is my make-up artist, Fadi Fawaz my hairdresser, Sophie Tafrishi, who is an absolute godsend, is first and foremost one of my best friends, but also my beautician who does my make-up and helps me with my frantic dress changes on tour; and Sean Joseph is my personal trainer.

*   *   *

It took about six months before Universal Classics and the lawyers finally got the contract together and ready at last for my signature on 23 March 2003. In the normal course of events I am a reasonably patient person, but when the contract kept going back and forth between the two sets of lawyers, I became very edgy and couldn't understand why it was taking so long. As ever, I was in a hurry to get going and so much of the seemingly endless nitpicking seemed to me to be a waste of precious time. Meanwhile, I was bursting to tell Nanna and my aunties and uncles and close friends. True to my original decision, though, I hadn't told anyone except Steve, Mum and Laura. In fact, until the moment I had the signed contract in my hand, it still felt unreal and I still felt it could be snatched from me. I honestly didn't know a moment's rest or feel secure until the day I finally went into the offices of Universal Classics and signed my contract.

A photographer, who was also present that day, took some photos for *Music Week*, the industry's magazine, and it was at that moment, while I was being photographed, that I realised it had happened: my dream had come true—I was going to make an album.

One day, not so very long after that, and certainly after the news had hit the press, the doorbell rang at the flat. When I went to answer it, a journalist from one of the tabloids was standing on the step, requesting an interview. (I learned later that Linda, my press agent, had not given out my address but the journalists have their own ways of finding out such things for themselves. Colleagues at the school where I was teaching, I then discovered, had already been contacted and asked how they felt about my record deal, and how the students felt about it—and they were all so unstintingly generous in their responses.)

'Bloody marvellous,' was what my colleagues said to me, and 'Well deserved, Katherine. You've worked hard enough for it.'

Everything happened so fast; it was breathtaking. All of a sudden, the news of what was described as my 'million-pound record deal' was everywhere. Then, when I drove home to Wales to celebrate with the family and was asked to do my first interview at Swansea Sound, my local radio station, the presenter, Kevin Johns, introduced me as 'Neath's richest woman, Katherine Jenkins'.

'Hey, hold on a minute,' I protested, laughing. 'I haven't received any money yet—and I haven't even paid off my student loan.' It was true.

By then I knew the money was going to be divided between six albums, because the artist pays to make the albums, and that by the time the money from the sales of these had been divided up and apportioned, it would probably be even more than the million pounds that was currently being bandied around. Until then, though, most of the money would go towards the cost of making the albums and not into my bank account.

It might sound daft, given how much I had wanted my dream to come true, but when I first realised I had the opportunity to do what I am now doing I found it quite hard initially. Having come from such a stable, well-ordered background—and being a Cancerian—I like stability, and a nine-to-five job with a pension would probably suit me best. It took me a while to get used to the fact that, although I now had a contract, the life I would be living in the future would be that of a freelance; and, as most freelances will confirm, that can be a hazardous hand-to-mouth existence. My mum was her usual sensible self, though, and just said: 'Always have a back-up plan, Katherine— something to fall back on.' I now give that advice to young people who come to me and talk about taking up singing as a career. Teaching was, of course, my back-up plan.

Meeting the press, I'd discovered straight away, was always a baptism by fire, and that's how it was for me. The journalist who door-stepped me, and the journalists who phoned everybody who knew me, were my first experiences of how quickly things can snowball and get out of hand. Soon after this, Universal sent me on a media-training course, but the guy who was in charge of the course said to me, 'You don't really need this, Katherine.' What he meant, I think, is that media training is mainly about encouraging people to talk and, as he discovered, I certainly didn't need that!

Some of the press coverage was hilarious. One

journalist, for example, described me as 'bubbly but gentle, a kind of wide-eyed Bambi on speed'; the *Sun* labelled me 'Pavatotti', and others suggested I would 'do wonders for the stuffy image of opera'.

*   *   *

People weren't calling the kind of music I wanted to do cross-over then. That came later; and more recently it's been called 'popera'—a term I can't stand. I was so excited to be making an album, and I was convinced there was a niche for somebody like me to do what I wanted to do, and make classical music much more accessible to people who had always felt opera was not for them. It had always frustrated me that so many people thought opera was out of their league. Where I came from, my singing teacher had had the good sense to introduce it to me at just the right time in the right way and I'd loved it from the start. Now I wanted to do this for others. After all everybody knew some operatic arias, even if they had only become aware of these through commercials or the soundtracks of films; and most knew bits of *Carmen* and *Madame Butterfly*. In fact, they probably knew a lot more than they realised. I wanted to tap into that, to take classical music to places where nobody expected it to go. It didn't have to be Covent Garden—I could sing at the Millennium Stadium, Cardiff, or a 400-seat church in the Highlands of Scotland.

It wasn't that I loved Wales any the less. I was proud to be Welsh, loved our history and traditions and our sense of pride in its beauty. It was just that I wanted my voice to reach millions and touch

114

people everywhere. I also wanted to see the world, visit places I hadn't even dreamed of visiting. I was twenty-three years old and the world, it seemed, really was about to become my oyster.

NINE

PERFECT PITCH

I couldn't wait to get into the recording studios to prove myself, and for *Première*, which I chose as the title for my first album, I included songs such as 'Questo è per te' ('I Do It For You'), 'Ave Maria', 'Habenara' from *Carmen*, 'Cymru fach' ('My Dear Little Wales') and 'Cym Rhondda' ('Bread of Heaven'). My amazing singing teacher, Beatrice Unsworth, helped me with the vocal arrangements.

When I recorded 'Questo è per te', I was very nearly overcome by emotion. I was singing it for two people: for my dad, because I knew I was going to dedicate the album to him; and for Steve, because he had played such a big part in my getting the record deal, had been my sounding-board throughout and remained so supportive during the days that followed. I could, anyway, have been forgiven for feeling so emotional about everything. This was a particularly edgy time for me because I had no way of knowing then if this recording would be just a one-off—I so wanted to stay the course and make more albums.

I loved singing in the recording booths at the studios. I had always been a perfectionist and wouldn't leave until I was sure the singing was up to my standard. Each album I've made is like a snapshot of the person I was at the time of making it. I can look back on each of them and appreciate that they sum up for me the different aspects of my life; and when I look at the album covers, I always

116

know exactly what was going on in my life—good, bad, happy, sad—at that moment. The songs they contain, and the covers that encase them, are private freeze-frame cameo moments that will be with me always.

*   *   *

When my first cheque arrived from Universal Classics, it had the logo of Universal Music printed at the top of it, and I kept picking it up and looking at it. I was so proud, so excited, and couldn't wait to go down to Barclays Bank to pay it in. But that proved to be a very damp squib.

The cashier looked at the cheque, looked at me, looked at the cheque again, then said in a very suspicious voice, 'Why have *you* got a cheque for so much money?'

I was really put out by her attitude and the wary way she was looking at me, and all my previous excitement died down. I also thought her question was very cheeky and that she was taking advantage of my youth. Things did not improve when she grunted: 'Are you the person named on this cheque? Can you prove you are?'

'Excuse me,' I replied, my blood rising, 'I'm paying a cheque *in*, not drawing the money *out*!'

She started to settle down after that, but she had spoiled what should have been for me a very triumphant moment.

Strange though this might sound to some people, especially other youngsters, I didn't immediately rush out on a spending spree. I had far too many things to do and was definitely in 'driven' mode. I'd been warned that only one in twenty people with a record deal actually make it and are successful, so I was only too aware that nineteen of us were likely to be dropped. Although I'd got the cheque, I was thinking: 'Now, if I'm going to prove myself and not become one of the nineteen, the hard work must begin now.' There were so many important decisions to make, not least what songs to include on my first album. Perhaps it is a little sad that I didn't take some time out to celebrate, but as well as being excited, I was also somewhat overwhelmed.

What I did do was trade in my old banger for a little silver Smart car that I could use to ferry myself to and from the recording studios. The rest of the money I just left in the bank 'for a rainy day'.

*   *   *

When you grow up in Wales, rugby is a big part of your life; and you can't really live there without loving it. Come an international, everything stops, and I can't remember a time when I didn't watch an international game on TV. Every Saturday mum would go and buy some meat, and Dad would cook steak and chips, and then we'd all sit down and watch the international at home. Then when Kevin, my first boyfriend, used to play rugby for the local team, Bryncoch, I'd go and watch him play. I also watched the school's rugby team. When the Millennium Stadium in Cardiff was being built, which coincided with my first year as a student at the Royal Academy, Kevin would get tickets for the international games at Wembley. So, one way and another, rugby has always been in my blood—and when I was sitting in the stands in the midst of the

Welsh supporters singing 'Mae Hen Wlad Fy Nhadau' with all the passion I could muster, I'd dream that maybe one day I could lead the anthem on the pitch.

Anyway, thanks to all those visits to the games, when I was actually asked to sing the Welsh anthem, 'Hen Wlad Fy Nhadau', at a rugby match in the UK, just prior to the World Cup in Australia, I knew what to expect from an international— especially a Wales versus England game, the most competitive game of all, when 74,000 people are packed into the stadium and millions more are watching at home.

Although I couldn't have been more excited at the thought of doing this, I was so riddled with nerves that for the whole week before the game I couldn't sleep, was having nightmares, and was in a general state of panic. I gave a great deal of thought to what I should wear. I went shopping with Steve and bought a really cute little red, soft leather jacket, which I wore with a white vest, red belt, shoes and handbag and blue jeans. I just love the photograph that was taken of me in that outfit. I look so thrilled and excited and, although I recently gave the handbag to be auctioned for one of my mum's favourite charities, I'm determined to keep the rest of the outfit. Those clothes will act as a reminder forever of what was for me a very special day right at the beginning of my singing career.

Nowadays when I do it, I just wear my rugby shirt and jeans and what I call my Millennium Stadium platform-heel patent shoes. I'm so proud of feeling I'm one of the team and love wearing my rugby shirt and jeans. I always get a new, boy's size

27–29 rugby shirt every time I sing and I'm collecting them all so that one day I can send them off to be auctioned for charities.

The groundsman at the Millennium Stadium, by the way, can't stand it when I go on to the pitch in my platform-heel shoes. Every time he sees me, he says, a note of despair in his voice: 'Katherine, would you mind wearing flat shoes when you go on the turf?' 'I can't,' I reply, 'I don't own a pair of flat shoes.' But, to please him, I've developed what I call my 'Millennium Stadium walk', which means I walk on the balls of my feet and make sure my heels don't touch the ground. This does, however, give me a bit of a Marilyn Monroe wiggle as I walk out on to the pitch, but that's the only way I can manage that walk without falling over.

What I was expected to do on the day of the match, I discovered, was to stand at the top of the tunnel as the away team entered from their dressing-rooms on the left. Then, when I saw them go running down the tunnel, followed by the Welsh team running down from the right-hand side, I would walk out and sing the anthem.

Before the teams came out, I was reminded that there would be the usual traditional bouts of spectator singing; and, as they had a military band and a male voice choir on the pitch to get them going, they certainly wouldn't need any encouragement. On the day, true to form, just before the teams were due to come out, the spectators sang 'Bread of Heaven', 'Men of Harlech' and then broke into a rendering of Tom Jones's 'Delilah'.

On my first occasion, standing on top of the tunnel, I was getting more and more nervous, but when I heard 'Delilah' it somehow seemed to help me to relax. This, I reminded myself, was an opportunity I had dreamed of. I had always wanted to lead my country in the anthem out there on the pitch. Everyone, I reminded myself, wanted me to do well, so I should just go out there, give it my best and love every minute of it.

In fact, when I walked on to the pitch, everyone gave me such an amazing welcome, I threw back my head and gave the anthem my all. While I was singing, I felt so proud—proud of the team, proud of all the spectators, but mostly proud to be Welsh. It wasn't until after I sang the anthem and walked back into the tunnel that my legs started to give way beneath me. I can honestly say that nothing since then has ever been that bad. But it's not surprising I was so nervous the first time. Given how many people were packed into that stadium, it really was like being thrown in at the deep end—or perhaps I should say into a gladiatorial arena.

It was after I sang at that match that I received the invitation to go to Australia to sing at the Sydney Opera House with Max Boyce in November 2003 while the World Cup was in progress. Max Boyce, who comes from Glynneath, was a coal miner before he became a comedian/singer. He had huge success in the 1970s when his career coincided with the Welsh rugby team's dominance in the Five Nations Championship; and, from then on, he remained a Welsh hero, a legendary entertainer in Wales and one of my favourite people! So, for me, to get an invitation to go out and sing with him in Oz while the World Cup was on was just wonderful. I've always tended to gravitate towards funny people, because I love

121

laughing my head off; and when I met Max, he didn't disappoint me. I seemed to spend most of the time when I was around him in stitches—and that meeting came about only because Max had happened to hear me sing at the Wales versus England rugby match, then picked up on the rumours that I wasn't being allowed to come to Australia.

Brian loves to tell the story about how my actual trip to Oz came into being, and I'm going to let him do this in his own words:

'The first event I ever went to with Katherine after I became her manager,' he always kicks off, 'was the Wales versus England rugby game, which was a warm-up for the 2003 World Cup in Australia. This being her first appearance of what was to become many at the Millennium Stadium in Cardiff, she was totally overawed—then almost overwhelmed, too, when the crowd sang "Delilah" as she walked on to the pitch.

'Being an opportunist, I thought, it would be a good public relations opportunity for Katherine if she accompanied the Welsh Rugby team to Australia to sing before every one of their games there and I discussed this with Rupert Moon, the Millennium Stadium events co-ordinator and official of the Welsh Rugby Union.

'To put it bluntly, Rupert didn't say "no", which I took to be a "yes", and for several weeks thereafter I pursued him on this matter by telephone until he finally responded with the bad news that the Australian Rugby Union—the organisers of the World Cup—had made their own arrangements for the pre-match anthem singing.

'Call it serendipity, or something I had for

breakfast, or a mere slip of my tongue, but a story appeared in the Welsh media that Katherine had been snubbed by the Australian rugby authorities and that the Welsh rugby team were considering boycotting the games if they couldn't take their "mascot—their weapon of mass distraction" to Australia. Most of this story, of course, was more the product of my imagination than fact! And Rupert Moon was none too pleased, as it would, of course, take more than that kind of incident for a team to boycott the World Cup. All was not lost, however.

'A week or two later, I received a call from Chris Stuart, who was producing a TV show for BBC Wales from Australia called *Max Boyce Down Under*. (As Max Boyce was, and is, a Welsh national treasure, he had been commissioned by the BBC to perform at the Sydney Opera House during the Rugby World Cup and, as ITV had the rights to transmit the actual games, to send his reports on the games back to BBC Wales.)

'Anyway, when Max saw the story about Katherine not being able to go the Australia, just like the *Cinderella* story, he invited her to "the ball" and asked if she would like to perform in his show at the Sydney Opera House.

'Both Katherine and I jumped at this opportunity for her to make her live debut at the Sydney Opera House (not many artists can say they have done this); and we thought the record company would be thrilled by this opportunity. The only comment we got, however, was: "Why are you going to Australia? The album is not out yet!"

'Nevertheless, we went and Katherine sang six songs on the show, which were sensational, and the

BBC decided to put two of these into the main telecast, which achieved a forty-three per cent share of the market and still rates as one of the highest viewed Welsh TV programmes ever—and, in my humble opinion, was the first real step to Katherine becoming a superstar.

'PS: Without Katherine as their mascot at the game, Wales got trounced at the World Cup!'

Thank you, Brian. Now, back to me!

The Sydney Opera House, I'd been told before I set out on that never-to-be-forgotten trip, hosted four auditoriums, had the most fabulous acoustics, and, what's more, was one of the most instantly recognisable pieces of modern architecture in the world. Situated on Bennelong Point, which reaches out into the harbour, the view of the skyline of Sydney Harbour Bridge and the harbour and the Opera House itself, especially when seen from a ferry, is totally unforgettable.

The thought of being in a real opera house, though, where the world's most famous opera stars had performed, was what excited me most—even more so than the flight or being in Oz itself. My dad had spoken often to Laura and me about his time 'down under' when he was in the Navy, and he used to say that if he ever won the lottery, or the pools again, he'd take us on a family holiday there. Because he died while we were still so young, that never happened, but I would have given anything to take him there with me.

I felt emotional when I walked out on to the stage of the Sydney Opera House for the first time and looked down at an auditorium that seemed to be full of Welsh ex-pats. There was even a woman in the front row wearing full Welsh national costume. They could not have been more appreciative and responsive.

I stood there, a huge lump in my throat and tears welling in my eyes as I thought of my dad and remembered how much he had longed to take us there. It was one of those moments when I really had to have a little word with him: 'Please, Dad, help me to get through this'; and I know, without any doubt whatsoever, that it was thanks to him I got through it without breaking down completely.

Then, joy of joys, when the autumn rugby series started, the Welsh rugby team asked me to sing at their matches against New Zealand and Australia and, when I did, the ever-witty press continued to hail me as 'Katherine, the Welsh rugby team's weapon of mass distraction.' Becoming the team's mascot, though, was never an official thing; it just happened. In fact the press fellows were largely responsible for putting the team and me together—and I'm so glad they did. I really enjoy it and I now think of it as a special, much-loved job. On international days people are always saying to me, 'Are you on duty today, Katherine?'

These days, I actually have a room named after me at the Millennium Stadium. I sing at every home game and make sure I organise my diary around those days. Just recently, I've also started to go to the away-game internationals and did my first one in Paris. Although I know some people believe I'm paid a fortune to do this, I actually do it for free—for the sheer love of the game, the players and Wales, and it's something I will continue to do for as long as the team asks me to.

'Fancy being among all those gorgeous guys,' people are always saying to me.

'It's a hard job, but someone's got to do it,' I reply.

What I love about rugby is that it's a gentlemen's game. The players are all so well mannered and quite shy in my company, which I like. They might wrestle with each other in scrums, and engage in the most brutal-looking tackles on the field, but afterwards they shake hands with their rivals and often go off to have dinner together. Sometimes, after a game, I have to rush off because of other commitments, but whenever I can I stay and socialise.

When I first see them at the various stadiums, they are obviously all het up and under a lot of pressure, so that's not a time for chitchat. Then, when I'm standing in the tunnel, they just run past me on to the pitch and I follow behind. Sometimes they have wound themselves up so much they can't even make any eye contact before a game.

When Welsh people hear the anthem, it stirs their hearts and sets the blood coursing through their veins; and when I hear 74,000 people singing it, it gets me every time. We always practise the anthem about an hour before the game in a huge car park below the stadium. We assemble: band, choir, Haydn James the conductor, me, and even the goat. It's my chance to get the emotion—and sometimes the tears—out of the way before I sing for real on the pitch.

If I'm ever lucky enough to become a mum and have boys, I will certainly encourage them to play rugby. No pressure, then!

* * *

126

I was so thrilled when *Première* was finally released. On the jacket notes I was determined to thank everybody who had played a part in inspiring me and bringing me to where I now was. I was only too aware that I owed a special thank you to my dad, who had always done so much for me; to my mum, who had planted the music seed in me and given me constant love and support; to Laura, who'd always been a brilliant sister and fantastic friend; and to Steve DuBerry who'd given me his time and energy and believed in me; to Brian Lane and the team at Bandana, the world's best management team; and, last but not least, to my boyfriend, Steve, who had given me all that he had to give, not least his heart, which was the biggest in the world.

All I wanted to do on the day the album was released was to rush from person to person, saying thank you, I love you so very much—and that included, of course, everybody at Universal Classics who had given me this chance to prove myself. To them, and to everybody else I loved, I just wanted to draw on the title of a song from my own album and say: 'Questo è per te'—'This is for you'.

Inevitably, after the initial high died down, the nail-biting began. Had I done enough? Could I have done more? Should we have included this or that song? The wait between the end of the recording and the album hitting the shelves had been agonising—and remained agonising until the news started to come in.

'All's well,' Brian, my manager, kept telling me. 'Your album is leaving the shelves as soon as it's placed there.'

That was good news enough. But then came even better news—news that I had never dared hope for or dreamed of receiving for my first album. *Première* had shot straight to the top of the classical charts.

It couldn't get better than that, could it? But, unbelievably, in the very near future, it did.

TEN

MEMORIES ARE MADE OF THIS

'So, Tinseltown's been calling you,' the newspaper reporter was saying, 'and recently you were in a film called *A-List*. Does this mean that now Hollywood has come knocking at your door you are going across the pond to make it big there?'

'No,' I replied, 'the *A-List* film happened purely by chance.'

At that time in 2003, Steve, my boyfriend, who is very handsome and has that square-jawed, film-star look, had had lots of offers to go to Hollywood and make films, but he was always too busy with his pop group, Worlds Apart, to follow them up. But after the band broke up and he was having a break from the music scene, he thought that maybe he'd go into acting and when he went to Los Angeles for an audition, I went with him—my first time to Hollywood.

When Steve and I arrived, we went straight to the Standard Hotel on Sunset Boulevard and had only been there twenty minutes when it was time for Steve to go for a meeting about the film. I sat there while Steve and the lead actor, Damon Shalit, were doing a read-through of the script and when they'd finished, the producers said they would love Steve to be in the film. Then, having spotted me sitting there, they said 'You've gotta be in the film, too.'

'No way,' I replied, startled. 'I'm just his girlfriend, here to give moral support. I'm a singer

129

not an actress.'

'Don't you sing opera?' one of the movie moguls asked.

'Yes.'

'Well, that needs acting skills.'

'Yes,' I said, doubtfully. 'But it's the music that moves me. I've no desire to act with words.'

'What if we make the part mute?'

And that's how, in the end, I agreed to take on a silent role in the movie, which involved me being in several scenes—and in one in particular where Steve was supposed to be in a coma and I was sitting next to him crying.

As this was a proper Hollywood production, with Sally Kirkland and David Carradine in the cast and more than twenty people on the set, I was terrified, wondering how on earth I was going to be able to act this coma scene out. But, when I walked on to the set for the start of the filming, I saw Steve made up as if he were desperately ill with all these tubes coming out of him, and I just burst into tears. I was genuinely crying because I was so upset at how ill he looked.

After the director called 'Cut', she turned to the others and said, 'Hey, guys, that's what real acting is all about.'

'Hmm!' I thought, but I decided not to disillusion her and the others by saying that my tears were genuine, not acting. The fact that it worked was a fluke and I have no plans to go into movies. In fact, I'm pretty sure I won't be doing anything like that ever again. It was just a one-off for the man I loved.

During the time we were in Hollywood, I'd more or less finished recording my first album *Première* and, as I had the first cuts with me, we kept playing it in the car when we were driving around. Hollywood! What a place to listen to one's first album.

*   *   *

Much as I enjoyed, and still enjoy, being in recording studios, there is nothing to compare with performing live. I adore being on stage, in front of an orchestra; love having that direct connection with the audience, and being able to make their eyes well up with tears when I'm singing or laugh when I'm larking around and talking. And it's impossible to become blasé because no performance, no audience, no day or night is ever the same.

I'd been doing live performances since I was four years old, but I'd never done the kind of performances I was being booked to do then on my first headline tour. Since releasing *Première*, I had entered a different league and was now considered a professional, somebody who could 'put bums on seats', which I still found hard to believe.

In October 2003, I was invited to sing at a special mass honouring Pope John Paul's silver jubilee at Westminster Cathedral. All cathedrals are special places, but the huge dome in this one really allowed my voice to soar as I sang Schubert's 'Ave Maria'. Afterwards, Cardinal Cormac Murphy-O'Connor, the leader of the Catholic Church in England, gave me a blessing.

I will never forget my first appearance at London's Royal Albert Hall, firstly because it has a gigantic auditorium; and secondly because of a totally unexpected event that nearly undid me. Up until that night, the most embarrassing moment of my career had occurred when I was singing at the Brecon Jazz Festival in Wales in front of two thousand people. As I started singing, the strap of my halter-neck dress suddenly pinged and slowly slid off from around my neck and I had to finish singing the song, praying that the dress wouldn't fall down altogether. It was a very long few minutes to the end of the song and I was dying of shame and embarrassment throughout, but at least it broke the ice and actually proved to be a great start to a concert when I turned to the audience and said: 'My mother's always telling me not to buy such cheap dresses!' That, then, remained my most embarrassing moment until my next most embarrassing moment during my first-ever appearance at the Royal Albert Hall.

In all my concerts I change dresses at least four times and, for this concert, I was wearing an enormous white gown that had been made especially for me. It had an enormous hoop under its skirt and was covered in Swarovski crystals. I adored it, but the first time I put it on in my Albert Hall dressing-room, the zip jammed, then broke. The lesson I learned too late that night was always to have a spare performance dress with you!

I did, as it happened, have a dress, but it wasn't what I had intended to wear for a performance and was by no means the big finale dress that I had planned to wear. Anyway, I had no choice. Having put on the dress, I went on stage and said to the audience: 'Well, you are never going to guess what has happened . . .' and when I told them they all burst out laughing. As Mum was leaving the Royal

132

Albert Hall afterwards, she heard one lady say to another, 'I bet she only said that to make us laugh . . .'

But for me it was just a case of overcoming my disappointment and honouring that old adage 'the show must go on'. In time one of the things I came to love about live performances is that you just never know what's going to happen and, when something unexpected does, you just think 'Oh well, memories are made of this' and get on with the show.

There are so many memorable things that occur to help you remember different performances, but I hope a pinged halter strap or jammed zip will never again put in an appearance at any of my shows.

After the release of my first album, I always made a point of going out to the foyer at the end of live shows to sign programmes and album covers. I loved meeting everyone and having a chat—and making a mental note of what they would like me to include on future albums. Sadly, as I became better known, those moments could not last. There were just too many people waiting—sometimes 3,000—and, as I couldn't bear to disappoint anyone or turn anyone away, I had to stop making these personal appearances in foyers. By then, usually I had to hit the road and head for the next venue anyway.

'What has been your strangest experience while promoting your albums or being on tour?' is a question interviewers often ask me these days, and two occasions invariably spring to mind.

The first was a signing in a record shop in Cardiff. When I turned up, there were only about fifty people waiting in the queue. As the first lady came up to me, she whispered, 'Katherine, would you sign this for my friend's husband?'

'Of course,' I said, 'what's his name?'

'The thing is,' she replied, dropping her voice lower, 'John's passed away, but he loved you, and loved your music, and we would like to put the CD in the coffin with him.'

My mind went completely blank. This was my first ever signing, and I was sitting there thinking, 'Oh, my God, why doesn't somebody teach you about such things!'—and I just couldn't think what to write.

'Shall I just write "With love from Katherine"?' I asked.

'Could you make it a little more personal,' she pleaded.

At that, I sat there for a good minute thinking: 'What on earth can I write?' then, very aware that other people were waiting, I wrote: *'Dear John, I hear you were a really great guy. Sending you all my love, Katherine.'*

The extraordinary thing is that this story has entered folklore. Since then, when I've been doing the rounds and signing, representatives from record companies have said to me, 'You know, I once heard of a girl who was asked to sign one of her CDs for a guy in a coffin.'

'That was me!' I chortle, adding, 'I really got thrown in at the deep end, but then those sort of things always seem to happen to me.'

My second strangest experience was when I was appearing on a Japanese TV show. On these shows, you never ever know what's going to happen. I was singing *Amazing Grace* and, just as I was nearing the end of the song, a man burst on to the stage dressed as Sid the Sloth, the character from the animated film *Ice Age*, and started dancing around like a lunatic behind me. It was live TV, but nobody had told me this was going to happen, and there I was singing my heart out as I approached the climax of a very emotional song. Well, there you go!

*   *   *

I might be a performer, but I've never been an exhibitionist, and, when I am not performing, I'm actually quite a shy person, which is why I found the first time that Universal Classics invited me to be their guest at a red-carpet event for the 2003 Classical BRIT Awards a total nightmare. (BRIT stands for The British Record Industry Trust.)

This is the most prestigious event in the classical music industry's calendar, and all the proceeds are donated to charity. Millions have been raised over the years for the BRIT School for Performing Arts and Technology and Nordoff-Robbins Music Therapy. So, for me, this invitation was a very important one. In the car on the way there, though, I was in such a state I couldn't breathe. Universal had hired a stylist for me who had got me this dream of a gold dress that I absolutely loved, so I was all dolled up for the event; but I was convinced that when I stepped on to the red carpet in front of all the onlookers I would feel like a total unknown because, having made only one album, nobody would have a clue who I was.

I was right to be nervous. Things certainly got worse before they got better, but not for the reasons I had anticipated. When I got out of the car—always difficult when you are trying to arrange your dress nicely—and started to make my way up the red carpet, I was completely overwhelmed, nearly washed away by the greetings from the crowd. Onlookers and photographers surged forward, shouting my name, which was both deafening and daunting. I didn't know how to react or where to look. There were about forty photographers in front of me and people on both sides of the carpet, some on ladders, yelling: 'Katherine, over here', 'Katherine, this side, this side'.

I did my best to please everybody, looked this way, then that, tried to keep smiling on command, but it was impossible to satisfy everybody. There were also so many things I was trying to bear in mind. 'Hold your tummy in,' I was thinking. 'Keep your shoulders back;' 'Keep a nice big smile on your face;' 'Is the dress as it should be?' 'Am I posing in the best way to show it off?'

Meanwhile, the crowd was getting more and more frantic: 'Here—here—over here'. It was totally manic and, in the end, I didn't know where to look. Nobody teaches you how to deal with this kind of situation and I was stunned. How did so many photographers know my name? I was absolutely amazed, and part of me remained all of a tremble throughout the evening.

I really am very shy if I do not have a particular function, like singing, and I don't think many people realise that, especially as I have always been such a chatterbox. But I can feel very overcome when I walk into a room to meet forty-plus people, or meet people who come backstage to see me.

When I am nervous my heart starts to pound, I become short of breath and I giggle. Usually in these kinds of situations, I throw myself into things, but I feel very vulnerable. That red carpet, the first time I attended the BRITs, I can tell you, seemed like a very, very long walk.

Once inside, having started to breathe normally again, I settled down and thoroughly enjoyed the event and the party that followed. I had to leave early that night, though, because Steve and I were going to Cannes for the film festival and had a very early flight the next morning. I remember getting up at some ridiculously early hour and then waiting for the flight to be called at Luton Airport. While I was sitting there, I noticed a man alongside me reading a morning paper. As I glanced at it, I thought, 'Oh, my God, that looks like me'—and it was.

I ran to W. H. Smith and bought all the papers I could lay my hands on. I was in every one—and the dress looked wonderful. That was fun, and it made all my previous night's suffering worthwhile. It was not to be the last time I would go through my own little hell and back for the BRITs.

ELEVEN

SIMPLY THE BEST

It's hard for me to believe now that there were only seven months between my recording and releasing my first and second albums, *Première* and *Second Nature*. When I made *Second Nature*, I wanted to be involved in as many aspects of the recording as possible, and I chose to go with my producer Nick Patrick to Prague, where the sixty-piece orchestra was being recorded in the Rudolfinium, where I'd been told Dvořák premiered his works.

I took my mum on this trip with me. There was such an exciting moment in store for us when we walked down a corridor of the Rudolfinium and heard the orchestra playing the music I was going to record on the album. For me, it was one of those 'Wow' moments that takes your breath away. All of a sudden, everything I had only heard in my head up until that moment came to life, and I thought: 'Oh, my God, this is really happening—this is my new album.'

It was thrilling, and I came back from Prague all fired up and energised, full of new ideas, thinking, 'Wouldn't it be lovely if I could record some of the tracks with the National Youth Choir of Wales.' I'd had such fun when I was a member of the choir and I remembered that during those days we sang on a TV show with Bryn Terfel, who was such an inspiration to me. At that time we had special little satchels for our music, which had National Youth Choir of Wales printed on them, and we all got them signed by Bryn. Recently, when I sang at a dinner that was being given in Bryn's honour, I couldn't resist saying to him, 'Bryn, you won't remember this, but when I was about sixteen you signed the inside of my satchel—and I've still got it among my treasures.' He didn't remember me, of course, but he did remember the occasion.

Having approached Keith Griffin, the choir's director, I went to Carmarthen, Wales, when the choir was attending a course at Trinity College and teamed up with them to record 'Vide Cor Neum', 'Calon Ian' and 'O Holy Night'. It was such fun being back with that choir, which holds a very special place in my heart. Their sound is so clear and clean and I'm so glad they could take part.

For *Second Nature* I also included some songs that had been suggested by fans when I was signing autographs, and the album also featured a number of my classical favourites, including 'Song to the Moon' (from Rusalka) and Mozart's 'Laudate Dominum'. Other highlights for me were 'Caruso', 'Aranjuez' and 'Time to Say Goodbye'.

I'd thought that releasing my first album would engender the worst attack of nerves I had ever experienced, but releasing the second was even worse—just awful. Having had such a success with *Première*, I hardly dared hoped I could pull it off a second time; but *Second Nature* entered the charts.

*   *   *

From *Second Nature* onwards, the actual choice of songs was mostly all down to me, and what I decided to include came about in a variety of different ways. Between recording the first and

139

second album, I'd become much more in tune with myself and able to choose songs I thought would be best for my voice. By then, I'd also been out on the road and met fans, who would come up to me after every show, and say: 'Please recor . . .' and I started making a list. Likewise, sometimes when I was watching a film, or listening to some background music being played in a restaurant, I'd start thinking, 'Gosh—that would be good on an album.'

So by the time I came to record *Second Nature* I had pages and pages of songs to choose from, which I then took to the record company so we could go through them. Then, having done this, I made my decision. I thought it was only right the decision should be mine—after all, I was the one who had to sing the songs, hopefully for many years to come, and I didn't ever want to become bored with what I was singing. I also felt I understood my fans better: I was the one who was at the coalface, so to speak, and in touch with them.

Usually when I perform a song live for the first time, my focus is on the technical side of things. But when I have performed it a number of times, the actual technique goes into auto-pilot—muscle memory, my singing teacher Beatrice calls this; and as I know by then what I have to do technically, I can really let rip and get into the emotion of the song.

This reminds me, I was once told that a fan had said he would pay treble the price of his concert ticket if I would sing Carmen's 'Habanera' when drunk. But I had to disappoint him: I would never go on stage tipsy.

I realised very early on that, like most performers, I was a very superstitious person, especially about my routine when about to go on stage. At these times, everything has to be done in a certain order. I always do my hair first, never put shoes on a table, have to have Kylie's *Greatest Hits* playing—and, if there is a choice of toilets, I always use the same one. Even if that toilet is busy, I have to wait, and I can't explain why. Barrie, my stage manager, always makes me a special drink when I am on tour. Made fresh every day, this is a mix of freshly juiced pineapple, Manuka honey and ginger, which he warms up. It's really good, relaxes my vocal cords, and now I can't do without it. Likewise, I always have to say *'Tuoi-tuoi'* to the orchestra and to my musical director and conductor before I go on. I haven't a clue what this expression means or where it originated from, though. It's just something that's said in the classical world.

I knew from a very young age that my voice was a gift that I should never abuse, and I feel I have made a good job of looking after it. I'm not totally obsessed with wrapping a scarf around my throat at all times like some singers, but I do try to rest my vocal cords and keep as calm as I possibly can before a concert. Sometimes when I am on tour and doing a lot of back-to-back concerts, I don't speak at all between performances and just use sign language.

I also avoid smoky areas and do not allow people to smoke near me. If I get the slightest tickle or have a sore throat, I am not a happy bunny. I get very depressed if I can't sing properly; and I'm so happy when my voice is working at full power and in good form.

*   *   *

However happy and fulfilled people were feeling during the Christmas festivities of 2004, and over that New Year, the natural disaster of truly epic proportions that swept through Asia couldn't fail to dampen spirits and cast a huge shadow of grief over all of us. At least 220,000 lives were lost in that catastrophic tsunami and millions of people were left homeless and without access to safe drinking water or food, so vulnerable to disease.

At least some of our hearts were eased when we heard that, thanks to the immediate setting up of Tsunami Relief Cardiff, there was something we could do to help the survivors—and, along with many other performers, I appeared at the Cardiff Millennium Stadium for what proved to be the biggest charity concert since Live Aid twenty years before.

At the Tsunami Relief Concert, which added £1.25 million to the £200 million that had already been raised by the British public for the victims of the disaster, I performed alongside legendary pop stars, such as multi-Grammy-winning singer and rock guitar player, Eric Clapton, Jools Holland, the Manic Street Preachers and the Stereophonics. The organisers that night—Paul Sergeant, the Stadium's general manager and his team—were heroic. In the wake of the Boxing Day tragedy, they had put the concert together in just three weeks.

Before I walked out on stage, a five-minute montage containing footage of the disaster was played and then, fighting back tears like everyone else, I walked out and opened the concert singing 'Amazing Grace'. There were, I heard later, 60,000

142

fans packed into the stadium and millions more who joined us on TV, radio and online. It was an incredibly moving moment when the crowd, who seemed to stretch out forever on all sides of me, began waving LED torches that represented someone who had died as a result of the disaster and joined in my second song 'You'll Never Walk Alone'.

Throughout the concert, messages of goodwill were also read out from Prince Charles, politicians and celebrities, including Tony Blair and Wales's First Minister Rhodri Morgan, and Welsh rugby coach Mike Ruddock. I was so proud of Wales that night: it was such a good cause and we had shown we were capable of delivering at very short notice.

No doubt about it, that was a Boxing Day, New Year and concert that I will never forget; one that was a reality check that stopped us all in our tracks, helped us to get our priorities right, draw closer to our loved ones, count our blessings and appreciate what we had.

It was at the tsunami concert that I met Charlotte Church for the first time. We didn't really get a chance to speak, though, until later in the year when, along with Max Boyce, Charlotte and I were both asked to sing the Welsh national anthem at the Six Nations Grand Slam at the Millennium Stadium when Wales was playing Ireland. This was the final game of the tournament and the idea was to get the crowd singing to boost the team's confidence; and three voices were considered better than one to help Wales win the Six Nations Grand Slam.

From the moment I signed my record contract, tabloid journalists had been linking my name with

Charlotte's, which was not really surprising given that we were both young and Welsh; and when we shared a dressing-room that day, Charlotte and I hit it off at once while we were doing our make-up, warm-ups and getting changed. I really like Charlotte. She is such a lovely girl. Warm, funny and refreshingly honest. You can't help but like her immediately and I can tell you that despite her move into pop, she still has an amazing classical voice. Trust me, I've warmed up with her. I was so glad we got on so well because, before that, the journalists had kept implying that we were arch-enemies who hated each other.

'How can I hate somebody I haven't even met,' I kept protesting in those days. 'And I'd certainly never say anything bad about another girl from Wales who is doing so well.'

They also ranted on about whether I would ever, like Charlotte, venture into the pop arena. To this day, Charlotte and I remain good friends, who have made the following pact: if we ever read anything derogatory in the papers that one or other of us is supposed to have said about the other, we will both know that the journalists have made it up.

*   *   *

It was BRIT time again. To be reminded of that in Brian's office was excitement enough for one day, but there was more. I had been told by then that I was the only person in musical history to hold two consecutive number one positions, with *Première* and *Second Nature* in the classical album charts at the same time. But, in the next breath, Brian gave me yet more amazing news.

'Hold your breath, Katherine,' he said, with a beam that lit up the whole room. 'Both your albums have been nominated for the "Album of the Year" at the Classical BRIT Awards. You're up against yourself!'

'No way!'

I started jumping around. I was not thinking about winning, it was honour enough to be nominated, and I couldn't wait to phone Steve, Mum, Laura and Nanna.

'They won't believe this,' I kept saying to Brian as I dialled Mum's number.

'Who's a clever girl?' my mum said. 'Now you really are mega!'

Preparations for the Classical BRIT Awards that year, 2005, started for me about a month before the actual event. First I went to see dress designers, Lily and Dana Kruszynska, to plan my dress. By then, they had a life-size mannequin of me in their workshop, so most of the work could be done without my needing to be there. Nevertheless, I still went for lots of fittings to ensure that everything was perfect. Then I started making sure I would look my best by going for regular workouts at the gym, stopping eating chocolate, starting pampering my skin and trying out new hairstyles.

Getting ready for the BRITs is like a full-on military-exercise, and the closer we get to the night, the more everything starts to come together. Then it's a question of listening to Mum, Laura, my aunties and my friends talking about what they are going to wear or buy. And, sooner rather than later, we are all sorted and in BRIT mode.

What made that BRIT even more special was that my mum had made all the arrangements to bus forty members of the family and friends up from Neath to the Royal Albert Hall. Having arranged for them all to stay in a hotel near there, they got themselves all dolled up, ate in the restaurant at the Albert Hall then, complete with Welsh flags to wave plus some banners they had made, came to watch the event itself. So, there I was, proud as Punch, sitting at a table with my manager, Brian, and others on my management team, and the execs from Universal Classics and, of course, Steve, listening to all the nominations and album titles being read out, including 'Katherine Jenkins' *Première* and *Second Nature*'.

Then, unbelievably, and I really thought I had imagined it, I heard the words: 'And the winner is . . . *Katherine Jenkins—Second Nature.*' Everything went into super-slow motion. For a moment, I thought I was going to stop breathing— then I just burst into tears at the table.

One of the reasons I was so astonished is that you can usually tell at the last moment if you are going to win because, just as the nominations are being read out, a cameraman moves into position to get a close-up of the winner, so that when he or she gets up and walks towards the stage to collect the award, they are able to walk backwards in front of the winner and get the footage.

The Classical BRIT, however, so wanted a natural reaction from me that they put a dummy camera in front of Sir James Galway; and, when I saw the camera in front of him, I actually turned to Brian and Steve and said: 'See, I told you, James Galway would be the winner,' just as Classic FM's Simon Bates announced, 'The winner is Katherine Jenkins.'

146

Struggling to my feet, I began the long walk towards the stage and, as I went past my mum in the front row and the rest of the Taffia, who were frantically waving their flags, I could see Mum going mental. She leaned over to grab my hand and, at that point, I completely lost it. I was crying hysterically and thinking, 'Oh, my God, what am I going to say? Please don't let me forget to thank anyone.'

It was all so surreal, so emotional—and, since then, I have had every sympathy with anyone at the BRITs or Oscars who goes completely to pieces. When I made my brief speech, I dedicated the award to my dad and said 'Everyone here means something to me tonight, and the only person who's not here is my dad, but, in truth, he is here, so this is for him.'

After the award ceremony, I had to go to the press room where the journalists were waiting and I took that opportunity to praise all the generous, talented people I worked with, who'd supported me throughout the year and who were present to cheer me on that night—and that included, of course, all my family and friends. Then afterwards, at the celebratory party at the Zeta Bar in the Hilton, Park Lane, I stopped worrying about my throat becoming dehydrated and, for the first time that year, let my hair down and enjoyed a sufficient number of drinks to give me a bit of a hangover the next day. It was a lovely way to end a perfect day.

TWELVE

FAB-LOUS

Manic seemed to be the order of my day—every day. In addition to all the promotional work I was doing at that time, I had to get on with the preparations for a classical extravaganza that I'd been booked to appear in at Plymouth Pavilions in December. There I would be joining up with Aled Jones, whom I had adored ever since I heard him singing, 'Walking in the Air'.

Aled Jones, another of our Welsh home-growns, is *gor-geous*. I'd first met him in Tenby when he invited me to go along as his special guest while he was doing a concert tour. On that occasion, I was in my dressing room chatting to my mum when he came in to introduce himself. Contrary to his angelic looks, he is a really good laugh with a wicked, mischievous streak and loves to shock. I always enjoy his company.

So, all in all, I could not have been luckier: in just the few months that had whizzed by since I released my first and second albums, I had been on tour and really felt as if I had learned more about my singing and stagecraft in that short period than I'd ever done before. I'd also had ample opportunities to perform live in front of huge audiences and now had a much better idea of what worked and what didn't.

Two hundred thousand people, bless them, had bought my first album *Première*, and made me 'the fastest selling soprano of all time', and 480,000 people had bought my second album, *Second Nature*.

There was just one problem I would have loved to resolve. I was still so overcome when people praised or clapped me at the end of a performance that I was reduced to giggles because I never quite believed all this was for me. I know some performers 'milk' the applause, but I couldn't wait to get off stage because such moments always left me overcome by shyness.

'Katherine,' Brian kept pleading with me, 'please take a longer bow.'

'I can't, Brian,' I kept replying. 'It's not that I'm unappreciative, I just don't know how to react to all that applause.'

And, believe it or not, despite everybody, most of all Steve, who tried to boost my confidence, that remains a problem.

*   *   *

After I took part in the Tsunami Relief Concert in Cardiff, the organisers of Live 8 invited me, along with other pop singers and groups, to take part in their shows. Live 8 was organised, of course, by the legendary Sir Bob Geldof and was going to be a series of concerts that would take place simultaneously in G8 states and in South Africa, and would be timed to precede the G8 Conference and Summit that was being held at the Gleneagles Hotel in Scotland, in July 2005.

Designed to support the aims of the UK's Make Poverty History campaign and the Global Call for Action Against Poverty, it was hoped that the shows would pressurise world leaders into

149

cancelling the debt of the world's poorest nations, increase and improve aid to those in need, and negotiate fair-trade rules in the interest of poorer countries. And it was with this aim in mind that ten simultaneous concerts were to be held on 2 July and one on 6 July 2005. More than a thousand musicians performed live at the concerts, which were also broadcast on 182 television networks and two thousand radio networks.

I couldn't think of a better cause and readily agreed to take part in the Live 8 shows in Berlin on 2 July and in Edinburgh on 6 July.

While the classic line-up of legendary stars were making ready in Hyde Park, London, I arrived in Berlin to perform 'Amazing Grace' a cappella (unaccompanied). This was the first time I had ever performed in Germany and I was absolutely thrilled that it was under the umbrella of the G8. As a classical artist, I would have thought my chances of being involved in such a huge global rock/pop concert were nil. But, no, I had been asked.

Being there, then, was mind-blowing. Germany is very much into rock music and back stage that day I remember seeing Green Day, Die Toten Hosen and a-ha. All these men were dressed in their customary black and wore black eyeliner, which was such a contrast to me as I had chosen to wear the most colourful, knee-length, off-the-shoulder dress that it was possible to buy. I looked like a human rainbow in all those eye-dazzling bright colours!

Meanwhile, back in the UK, London's Hyde Park had Paul McCartney and U2 opening the concert playing 'Sgt Pepper's Lonely Hearts Club

Band', followed by Pete Doherty joining Elton John for a version of T-Rex's hit 'Children of the Revolution', and Bob Geldof deciding on the spur of the moment to perform the Boomtown Rats' hit, 'I Don't Like Mondays'. But we, too, were having a *fab-lous* time in Berlin.

There was a great atmosphere that afternoon. As I walked out on to the stage, there were an estimated 250,000 people stretching from the front of the stage right up to the Brandenburg Gate. Just to see all those people, fanned out as far as the eye could see, was awesome, and I kept thinking, 'How on earth can they see me?' I certainly couldn't see where they finished: they just vanished from view in the far distance.

I was so nervous and wondering: 'How, after all the deafening high-energy rock music, will I go down with this crowd?' But I needn't have worried. As I started singing the opening line of 'Amazing Grace' the crowd fell instantly silent.

'Oh, gosh,' I thought, 'is this quiet a good or bad sign? Are they liking it, or has my operatic voice just stunned them into silence?'

But I need not have worried. As I finished singing, there was the briefest of pauses, just long enough for me to wonder if I was about to be pelted or lynched, followed by this incredible sound that hit me like a gi-normous wave as the crowd broke into applause.

After my performance, the day became one of the most manic I have ever known. Having done my piece, I literally jumped off the stage into a waiting car, which took me and Damon Field, from Bandana, plus my hair and make-up team Lee and Sally, straight to the airport where British Airways

151

had very kindly held a flight for us. The plane flew us to Heathrow, where we had a car waiting to take us straight to Hyde Park.

Then, almost before I had time to catch my breath, I was backstage there with the likes of Sir Bob, Snoop Dog, Annie Lennox, Madonna, George Michael, Coldplay and The Who.

'Oh my God,' I kept thinking. 'I can't believe I'm actually a part of this.'

Berlin had been awesome but now, backstage in Hyde Park, everybody I could possibly have wanted to catch a glimpse of was just walking around, including David and Victoria Beckham, Robbie Williams and Bono. In fact, backstage at Live 8 was the best showbiz party I have ever been to.

I was gutted that Brad Pitt had left by the time I arrived, but at least I saw George Clooney, which made up for it. In fact, everywhere I looked that night there were legendary stars and, as the backstage area was quite small, it was wall-to-wall with people I admired and respected.

It became even more surreal. While I was waiting to be interviewed by the BBC, Madonna walked in, accompanied by four burly minders, and sat down on the couch in front of me. She was the one person I had really wanted to see perform and, luckily for me, as the show was running late and the running order had changed, I did manage to see her perform 'Like a Prayer' and 'Music'. If the event had gone according to plan, though, I would still have been in the air flying to London when Madonna was singing those numbers.

What was tragic, though, was that, because I had a concert the next day, I had to leave for home immediately after my press interview, and was in bed by ten o'clock.

Long before the G8 conference events had come into being, I had been asked to sing at the Newmarket racecourse, and this invitation had been accepted and entered on my schedule. That was no problem until—news to me!—an announcement was published in the *Evening Standard,* alongside a picture of me, stating that the Final Push G8 concert was to be held in Edinburgh and that I would be singing there. Nothing that I would like better, and I really wanted to do it: the problem was nobody had actually asked me, so the event was not entered on my diary!

Anyway, when all this became apparent and the G8 organisers were told I had a prior commitment, they said: 'What if we put you on later in the show? Would there be any chance, then, that you could do both concerts and get to Murrayfield in time?'

Well . . . where there's a will, there's a way, they say, so, having said yes, it was all go-go-go. I had to go up to Edinburgh the day before the concert for the rehearsal; then, on the actual day of the racecourse concert and the G8 concert, I flew by private jet from Edinburgh to an airfield near Newmarket, Suffolk, where I was met and driven to the racecourse. Then having done the show there, I left and climbed on to a little four-seater helicopter that flew me back to where the private jet was waiting, then flew all the way to Edinburgh, where I had a police escort to Murrayfield Stadium.

The moment I arrived, I ran into the stadium, passing George Clooney on the way, and had just sufficient time to do my hair and get my dress on before walking out on stage to sing 'Nessun Dorma'. This was the first time I had ever

153

performed that aria live and the 60,000 people in the stadium went ballistic because it's such an emotional song.

What a day that 6th of July proved to be. Private jet, helicopter, police escort, complete with flashing lights all the way. I really did feel like a rock star. The Murrayfield Stadium concert, held at the venue closest to the actual location of the G8 Summit meeting, proved to be a great climax to the rally and, like me, many of the artists who had performed at the other concerts arrived to perform there, too.

On 8 July, when the G8 Summit ended, it was announced that leaders had pledged to increase aid to developing countries by US$50 billion overall by the year 2010, including an increase of US$25 billion in aid for Africa—and dear old Bob Geldof thanked the G8 for meeting the Live 8 goal.

All in all, Live 8 was a brilliant, memorable event that gave the poorest of the world real political muscle for the first time, and I was thrilled to have played a small part in 'making poverty history'.

*   *   *

What a year 2005 was turning out to be. Before I knew where I was I was asked to perform at the VE celebrations in Trafalgar Square, a 'Party to Remember', hosted by the BBC presenters Natasha Kaplinsky and Eamonn Holmes. This was a huge concert to mark the sixtieth anniversary of VE day and, much to the consternation of the pigeons, 15,000 people gathered in the famous square, overlooked by Admiral Nelson.

Singer Katie Melua began the show with her version of the World War II favourite 'White Cliffs of Dover', and Cliff Richard, Daniel Bedingfield and Will Young were among other singers who performed while Christopher Eccleston of *Doctor Who* fame and actor Richard E. Grant did some readings.

The square was filled with veterans and their families, and there was a lovely atmosphere. Determined to dress up in 1940s-style fashion, I wore a sparkly pink number, had my hair done in a style from that period, and went on stage early in the show to sing a song I really love, the unforgettable 'Ev'ry Time We Say Goodbye', made internationally famous by Ella Fitzgerald.

The concert also featured some footage of the original Trafalgar Square VE Day celebrations and Dame Vera Lynn, the wartime singer and 'Forces Sweetheart', made a special appearance that day. I'd been told that Dame Vera, who no longer sings in public, was going to be there and would be interviewed by Eamonn and Natasha and would then leave the stage just before I came on to sing the final song of the show.

When I went on stage, though, and was about halfway through singing 'We'll Meet Again', I noticed that Dame Vera was standing in the corner at the back of the stage, singing along with Eamonn.

'Oh, gosh, this is so wrong,' I thought. 'This is Dame Vera's song. She should be out here, centre stage. This is her moment.' In the next breath, although I thought I would get in trouble with all the TV cameras present, and that the TV station that was televising the event would go nuts with me for improvising, I went over to Dame Vera, took her by the hand and drew her out to the middle of the stage. I then sang the rest of the song with her holding my hand. It was such a lovely, spontaneous moment, and the people in the square went crazy as they looked up at and saw us holding hands—and then all the confetti came floating down. It couldn't have been a more emotional finale and afterwards, backstage, when both Dame Vera and I were overwhelmed by the reception we had got and were in tears, I said: 'Dame Vera, I really hope you didn't mind me doing that. I hadn't planned to drag you centre-stage, but I just felt it was the right thing to do.' She agreed it was a very special moment.

Later, so many people wrote to me thanking me for 'what you did with Dame Vera' and photographs of Dame Vera and me holding hands were featured in all the newspapers. All this confirmed for me how very dear Dame Vera was to so many who had lived through those terrible war years and how close they had always held her in their hearts since. Then, bless them, they paid me a very great compliment by beginning to call me the 'new Forces' Sweetheart'—something that, at that time, I had no idea would be responsible for involving me in so many adventures with some dangerous life-threatening consequences en route.

THIRTEEN

LIVING A DREAM

Living a dream? Was I? Absolutely—and that's how my third album acquired that title; a title that summed up what I had been doing, and all the momentous things that had been happening in my life. That didn't mean that I wasn't working harder than I'd ever worked in my life, because I was—and sometimes I hardly knew if I was coming or going. Nevertheless, I was then, still am, literally living a dream, having the best of times, and, aside from moments of sheer exhaustion, loving every minute of it. I certainly didn't take any of it for granted and I wanted all the people who bought my albums to know that I was really grateful for their continued support and that I couldn't have done it without them.

The choice of *Living A Dream* as the title for my third album, though, did not happen without a great deal of discussion. Initially, lots of titles were put forward, but I wasn't really happy with any of them. Then, one day, I heard somebody say to Damon Field who was working with us, 'How are you doing?' and he answered, as he always did, 'Living the dream, thanks—living the dream.' That was the moment it first occurred to me that *Living A Dream* would make a great title for my album. After all, what could be more appropriate? I was!

By then, I had come to appreciate how very easy it would be to start putting on airs and graces and going down the slippery slope to becoming a prima donna. This is too easy when there is always someone offering to do something for you, and some people almost expect that kind of behaviour: 'What would Miss Jenkins like in her dressing-room?' I could, if I wish, say, 'Four puppies to play with, a large bowl of only blue Smarties and the entire room to be filled with fragrant lilies.' Yes, it would be very easy to be like that, but I was determined never to behave in that way; and I know, if I did, my mum would kill me!

*　　　*　　　*

By the time *Living A Dream* was ready to be released, so many extraordinary things had happened to me, I am almost at a loss for words to sum up that period—things just kept going from unbelievable to even more unbelievable.

When *Living A Dream* hit the shops I was told, and I quote, I had 'become the fastest-selling classical artist ever—racking up more sales in the first week than Maria Callas, Placido Domingo, Luciano Pavarotti—and any other classical artist'. *Living A Dream*, it was being reported everywhere, had made me the fastest-selling soprano of all time.

There was yet more good news to come. When the charts came out, I heard that I now held positions one, two and three in the classical music charts with *Première*, *Second Nature* and *Living A Dream*.

The first track I'd chosen to put on my *Living A Dream* album was 'I Will Always Love You', a song that everybody associates with Dolly Parton—and therein lies a story. When I said I would love to sing this number in Italian on my album, Brian,

158

never one to let the grass grow under his trainers, said, 'Okay, I'll write to her, enclosing a track of you singing the song, and we'll see what she says; see if she'll give permission for you to record it.'

'That's a bit cheeky,' I thought.

Amazingly, though, having listened to the track, Dolly said, 'Yes.' I was so thrilled, so touched, and I first sang my Italian-language version entitled 'L'Amore Sei Tu' when I performed live at Nostell Priory, West Yorkshire, on 28 August 2005.

Among the other numbers on my *Living A Dream* album were some of my all-time favourites and some that had been suggested by my fans. These included 'One Fine Day', a deservedly eternal favourite from *Madame Butterfly*, 'Nessun Dorma', made unforgettable by the three tenors, Pavarotti, Domingo and Carreras, on the eve of the FIFA World Cup Final in Rome in 1990, 'All Things Bright and Beautiful', which I'd been singing since my choirgirl days, and the absolutely heart-rending aria 'Mon coeur s'ouvre a ta voix' from *Samson and Delilah*.

*　　　*　　　*

Something that never ceases to amaze me is the amount of fan mail I receive and I find it really humbling. It seems to increase every time I release a new album or do another live performance. The fans have always been full of ideas about the kind of songs they would like me to include on my albums, and I've always been very keen to respond to their suggestions and am determined to remain accessible to them. The last thing I want to be is the kind of celebrity who employs somebody to send out signed standard letters to the people who write to me. I get loads of fan mail, but I answer every letter myself, even though this takes hours. I've always thought it's really lovely of people to take the time and trouble to write a letter to me, and that it's only right that I should send a personal note back on the requested photograph. After all— and I cannot say this too often—it's the support of my fans that's got me to where I am today.

Universal Classics tells me that around two-thirds of my fans are male, but looking around concert halls I think it's more like 60:40, which means there is not a massive gender difference.

Inevitably, along with everybody else who is in the public eye, I get lots of begging letters asking, for example, if I could, please, send £132,000 so that a particular person can buy a new house; and just recently I had a letter from a man who asked for £200, so that he could go on a caravan holiday.

I also get really sweet letters, at least twenty a week, from all over the country, saying, 'When you're in our area, please pop over for a cup of tea and some home-made cake, and we'll sit down and have a lovely chat', or 'Next time you're in x, y, z doing a concert nearby, please pop in and stay the night.' I'm always so touched by such invitations. One letter that made me chuckle, though, was from a lady who I suspect was on her parish church council: 'We have just had a new toilet installed in the parish and we would love you to come and open it,' she wrote. She was quite serious, but I couldn't begin to imagine the kind of graffiti I might attract if I did what she requested. Fortunately, I was in the middle of a tour, but I did write to them wishing them luck.

160

I also get lots of marriage proposals. I always write back, but never refer to the proposal. I just say, 'I look forward to meeting you one day.' I get very shy when I read letters like that.

Some of the propositions are really funny, some are quite scary—freaky even—like the one that was delivered to our house in Wales. Written half in Welsh, half in English, it was full of biblical quotations that went on for twenty pages. Letters like that scare me because I don't understand what the person wants from me. I like to reply, but in these cases I have no idea what to say.

One proposal was from a man who enclosed photographs of himself dressed in white vest, slashed to the waist, *à la* Tom Jones, with lots of fuzzy hair sticking out of his chest. He had posed for this with his hands behind his head, leaning against the wall. There were quite a few variations of these pin-up pics, accompanied by a note that said, 'Katherine, I really would love to take you out for dinner and marry you, and I've enclosed these pictures so you can see what I—and my chateau in France—look like.' The chateau, I must say, was impressive!

I also get sent dozens of poems, which I keep in a box. One lovely lady in particular sends me a specially written poem every time she reads that something good has happened in my life.

From day one, I have kept all the fan mail I've received. I regard each one of them as a reality check; and, one day, I hope to show them to my children and grandchildren. In fact, whenever I read my fan mail I realise how important it is—and I was particularly struck by a letter I received recently from a lady whose daughter is seriously ill

161

with cancer. The lady who wrote the letter told me about a visit she had made to Australia with her young grandson, who is obviously having a very hard time coping with his mother's illness, and how he kept ferreting away an album of mine that she had taken with her.

'Sometimes,' she said, 'I could hear him playing your album through the walls at three o'clock in the morning, and each time the album reached the last song, I heard him get out of bed and go to the CD player to put it on again.'

That kind of letter brings me out in goose bumps. I do sometimes forget in the middle of all the stress of travelling around, just how important such a gift is; and the thought that it can bring such comfort to others who are going through hell puts it all back into perspective. My fans really are extraordinarily generous—and I do so appreciate them.

A question that kept cropping up around the time I released *Living A Dream* was: 'What do you think of shows like *The X Factor*?'—and my answer never varied.

'I have mixed feelings about shows like that,' I kept saying. 'Personally, I love watching the early stages because some of the auditions are absolutely hilarious; and they do give people, who have no idea about the business, a chance to get exposure and sing for people like Simon Cowell. But I also worry about how long a career the winning contestants will achieve from the show; and from my experience in teaching I also realise it can encourage youngsters to think they can be famous for doing very little—or nothing at all.'

That whole way of thinking, which is very

common at the moment, does worry me. When I was a teacher, for example, I used to ask the children that age-old question 'What do you want to be when you grow up?' and so many would reply 'famous'.

'Famous for what?' I would ask, but they rarely knew the answer.

I really do think we should be making it clear to young people that being famous—rather than notorious for whatever reason—is all about hard work, determination, focus and dedication. They should want to be famous because they are good at something.

I really don't know if auditioning for *The X Factor* is something that I would have done. I grew up with no knowledge of the music business and had a very lucky break. Maybe if things had been different, I might have considered it. If I had, I would not have been worried about standing in front of Simon Cowell—he really doesn't scare me. I've just never believed he's the nasty person he pretends to be and I have huge respect for the way he markets his artists.

What does scare me is being in a small room full of very important people, especially other singers whom I admire. I find that much more scary than being in a huge concert hall where, often, I can't see any of the faces in the auditorium. For example, when I was asked to sing at a concert in Pontypridd, the part of Wales Sir Tom Jones is from, to celebrate his sixtieth birthday, I was terrified. He had not been told I was going to be there and, when he was on stage, talking to the audience, I appeared from the wings singing his favourite Welsh song 'Myfannwy'. I was so nervous that night because I honestly didn't know if he would be happy about my having been invited to do it; but he couldn't have been more charming.

About four years before this, I had taken all the women in our family to see him perform in another of his shows at Cardiff Castle and when he came on stage, we all freaked out. For his birthday concert, however, as well as listening to Sir Tom, I was singing as well. This just illustrates for me how quickly things can change—and it is one reason why, when interviewers ask me what I most love about life, I say 'Life itself! You just never know what is around the corner, what is going to happen next.'

That was certainly true then, but there were times coming my way in the not too distant future when I could have been forgiven for editing that reply and saying instead, 'Being alive, and staying alive, so I can continue living a dream.'

FOURTEEN

RIGHT ROYAL MOMENTS

I blush to recall this, but being in a toilet at Buckingham Palace just proved irresistible to somebody like me who loves to keep photographic records for my mum—and the children and grandchildren I'm hoping to have one day; and writing about auspicious moments has brought me to the fact that, thanks to my singing career, I seem to have had more than my fair share of right royal days as well as a quota of embarrassing incidents.

This was especially true the first time I went to Buckingham Palace on St David's Day when the Queen was hosting an evening reception. When I arrived at 'Buck House', my eyes as big as saucers, I was directed to the nearest cloakrooms and told: 'When you are ready, please come back upstairs and we will tell you where to go.'

Thinking I had about ten minutes to spare before everyone else arrived, I took off my coat and went down to the toilets, where I decided to ring Mum on my mobile and tell her what the Buckingham Palace toilets were like. Having had some fun doing that, I then got carried away and started taking some souvenir pictures on my mobile. Suddenly aware that time was passing, I decided I'd better go back upstairs.

'I'm Katherine Jenkins,' I said to the nearest official and, as I did so, his eyebrows shot up.

'Oh, Miss Jenkins,' he replied, a note of panic in his voice, 'we are going to have to rush you through. You are the last guest to arrive and the Queen is literally about to walk into the room.'

'Oh, God!' I thought, blushing.

There I'd been larking about in the toilets when there were twenty other people present with whom I could have been spending time. The official raced me through the palace, into the room and, somewhat flushed and out of breath, I joined everybody else in the line-up just in time.

'How awful,' I thought, 'if I'd missed my moment with the Queen while I was photographing the toilets. Mum would have killed me.'

As I stood in the line-up, I was lucky enough to have the opera singer Bryn Terfel on my left-hand side, the percussionist Evelyn Glennie on my right and Jamie Cullum, the jazz singer, was a few further down the line. When the Queen entered, she moved along the line, chatting to each of us in turn, and I heard her say to Bryn, 'Did you enjoy the opening of the New Millennium Centre in Wales?'

'Very much, Ma'am,' Bryn replied. 'Did you?'

'I thought it was lovely,' the Queen answered, 'but it did go on a bit. My train was waiting for me for over an hour.'

The really classic line I overheard, though, came from further along the line and involved Brian May who was standing next to Eric Clapton. Addressing Queen's Brian May, the Queen said, referring to the party at the Palace for her Golden Jubilee, 'Oh, yes, you were the one who was playing the guitar on my roof.' As she was speaking, my mind flashed back to June 2002 when Brian, in full rock-God-mode, performed 'God Save the Queen' on the roof of Buckingham Palace, while below an estimated one million people watched outside the gates, along the Mall and around Queen Victoria's Memorial, while 200 million people, including me, Mum and Laura, watched it on television.

Then, turning to Eric Clapton, multi-Grammy-winning singer/guitarist, the Queen said, 'Oh, yes, nice to see you. Have you been playing the guitar long?'

'Just forty years, Ma'am,' Eric replied and everybody just cracked up.

That item was featured on the news that night. I was stunned to be standing there in that line-up, and was so thrilled when the Queen stopped in front of me and said, 'Why is it that all the best singers come from Wales?'

'I think it's in the blood, Ma'am,' I replied. 'There's such a culture of singing in Wales—and we are never too embarrassed to join in. I also think it's something to do with our accent, which is naturally melodious.'

I really do believe that. For example, when singers are being taught to sing a lot of emphasis is placed on accentuating vowel sounds, and as the Welsh, like the Italians, do that quite naturally, it gives us a headstart.

Once the initial greetings were concluded, the doors to another room were opened and everyone gathered there, who had not yet been able to meet the Queen, were at last able to see her, and the mingling began.

It was just such a lovely occasion, with so many people I admired in the music business there. I don't care what anyone says; lots of people were trying to play it cool that night, but everybody was tickled pink and excited to be there.

For yet another right royal moment I was invited by the Duke of Edinburgh to go to St James's Palace for the fiftieth anniversary of the Duke of Edinburgh Awards. For this, there was a photo call involving one person from each year of the awards; and, after that had taken place, I was driven to Buckingham Palace to join the Duke and the Queen and seven other guests for lunch. However, it was not only what happened at the palace on that occasion, but when the invitation first came into the office, which cracked me up.

At that time, young Damon was still working in Brian's offices and one day, when we were all out, he took a call from an official at Buckingham Palace saying, 'Would Katherine like to come to lunch with the Queen and Duke of Edinburgh?'

What was Damon's nonchalant reply? I am not kidding: 'I'll have to check her schedule with her and get back to you.' And, true to his word, he did: 'Oh, Katherine,' he said as I entered, 'the palace called. They want to know if you can go to lunch with the Queen and the Duke of Edinburgh . . .'

'What did you say?' I gasped.

'I said I'd have to check your schedule with you when you came back.'

'No, Damon! You did not.'

'I did—I swear,' he protested.

Although my heart stopped for a moment, I thought it was hysterical.

By then I knew that a lunch was held once a month for people who had excelled in their field, and this time there was someone from the arts (me) and someone from the military, the Church, science and environment. The other person

168

present was Prince Charles's secretary.

Having been handed a pre-luncheon glass of wine, the Queen's eight guests were just mingling and getting to know each other, when the corgis came padding into the room. Now I am besotted by dogs, so I just fell on to the floor and was playing and rolling around with them when the Queen walked in, giving me a close-up view of her feet.

'Oh, my God!' I said, scrambling up, covered in confusion.

It was one of those moments when her riposte could have been: 'Don't you mean, "Oh, my Queen!"' but she just smiled gently and said: 'Hello Katherine, how are you?'

'Very excited to be here,' I burbled, 'and I love your dogs.'

'Are they pure bred?' the lady next to me asked the Queen.

'Well, actually, no,' the Queen said, her face breaking into a smile. 'They're a cross between a Corgi and Dachshund, so I call them the Dawgis.'

I just loved that moment. The Queen really does have a great sense of humour and can be very funny herself.

'Shall we have lunch?' she suggested a moment later; and we all followed her into a dining room with an oval table laid for the eight of us. I was seated next to the Duke of Edinburgh and opposite him was the Queen. As I was by far the youngest person at the table, I was feeling quite nervous.

'What have you got coming up?' the Queen asked me.

'The Royal Variety Show,' I replied.

'And how are the rehearsals going?'

Honestly, the Queen is absolutely brilliant at

putting people at their ease.

When we had finished the three courses, a plate with some gauze on top of it and a glass bowl full of water was placed in front of me. That did it! I sat there, flustered, thinking, 'Just as I thought I was doing so well . . .'

Now, I was under the impression my table manners were good, but I hadn't a clue what these items were for, and I was so embarrassed. Then while I was sitting there worrying about that, a waiter came round with a choice of grapes or peaches, so I chose a peach and sat there holding it in my hand. The Queen had obviously sensed my panic and was so sweet—she just looked across with an expression in her eyes that said 'Watch me' and, without drawing any attention to me, very discreetly showed me what to do, which was to wash the fruit in the bowl, then dry it with the gauze. Bless her.

As I sat there going through the motions myself, I was astonished, thinking 'Surely, the fruit's already been washed!'

Afterwards, I couldn't wait to call my mum, who is a huge fan of the royals, and tell her all about the lunch. She agreed with me about the washing of the fruit.

The Royal Variety Show that I had mentioned to the Queen was held in the presence of the Queen and the Duke of Edinburgh at the Donald Gordon Theatre, which is part of the Wales Millennium Centre in Cardiff; and, as it was such a special occasion, I bought a ticket for Laura and my mum. I ought to have known better.

Getting there on time turned out to be a bit of a nightmare for Laura. She had to do a full day's work before setting off and although she did this in time to get the train from London to Cardiff, her train got stuck behind the Royal Train pulling into Cardiff, which meant that she arrived late at the theatre and was refused admission.

'Everybody,' my distraught sister was told, 'has to be in their seats—and seated—before the Queen arrives. There's nothing for it, you'll have to wait now for the second half.'

'But Katherine Jenkins is my sister,' Laura wailed, resisting telling him it was all the Queen's fault she was late, 'and that means I will miss her singing as she's the first on.'

The official did not take pity on her, so she phoned Damon from my management team and, minutes later, Laura was allowed to creep in and watch me perform from the wings of the stage.

While she was standing there, watching me, she noticed a TV monitor at the side of the stage and realised that if she crept across there, she could sit with two other girls, who were seated on two of the three seats placed alongside it, and would have a much better view of my performance on the screen. And this, in all innocence, is what she did.

What she had not realised was that the two girls sitting there were two of that evening's performers, Catherine Tate of 'Am I bovvered?' fame, and one of her sidekicks; and, just as I finished singing, the three seats, which were actually on wheels, suddenly spun around to shoot out to the centre of the stage. And Laura, who so nearly ended up as an uninvited guest in Catherine's act, just managed to do one giant leap off her seat before it would have landed her in the middle of the stage. Mum and I had been worried about where she was so at

171

least we would have known!

As one of the first acts that night, I appeared with the Blue Man Group to perform Donna Summer's 'I Feel Love'. This was not an easy feat. I was wearing a dress made of neon lights and weighing twenty-five pounds. It was absolutely killing my shoulders and I had to dance in it, but the performance was fun and I did enjoy myself.

One of the Blue Man Group's sequences that night was to coat the comedian Joe Pasquale in paint, attach him to a pulley and swing him against a large canvas, so that, as a trio of 'mute' performers, covered in their customary blue grease paint, latex caps to give them bald heads and black clothing, they could perform their hilarious 'spin-art' skit.

I couldn't resist watching some of this in the wings with Laura, but I also couldn't wait to get out of that dress.

*   *   *

Along with the lovely veterans, who had taken me to their hearts at the VE Day celebrations in Trafalgar Square, journalists were beginning to dub me the 'Forces Sweetheart'. But I must confess this was making me feel rather uncomfortable. It was such a special thing for people to say, but I didn't want it to be just a nice title that was given to me, I wanted to earn it—and going to Iraq to sing for the soldiers struck me as something I'd really like to do. I did not have to wait long.

Having performed regularly for the Chelsea Pensioners and performed at a Festival of Remembrance, as well as at the VE Day celebrations with Dame Vera Lynn—something that had been screened to the soldiers in Iraq—I guess it wasn't surprising that I received an invitation from the British Forces Foundation (BFF) to go and entertain the troops in Basra; and I jumped at the chance. Where I come from, family is incredibly important and when the invitation arrived just before Christmas, I thought: 'Wouldn't it be nice to show all these guys and girls who are away from their families that they haven't been forgotten.'

BFF, I learned, was launched in 1999 on board HMS *President*, London, by Jim Davidson OBE, who is renowned as a hilarious and infamous X-rated Comic Master. Jim was the founder and vice-president, HRH the Prince of Wales is the Patron and Baroness Thatcher the President. The meetings are held at the Cavalry Club in Piccadilly, London. HRH the Prince of Wales writes: 'With ever increasing commitments overseas our soldiers, sailors and airmen can expect to spend even longer periods away from their homes and families—and maintaining their morale becomes all the more important.'

And Baroness Thatcher comments: 'We owe an enormous debt of gratitude to the men and women of our armed forces who are often called to serve in difficult circumstances around the world. If, through the efforts of this Foundation we can relieve some of the pressures under which they work, then we not only demonstrate our thanks to them but we also contribute towards the better efficiency and morale of those who serve this country.'

By the time I met Jim, who has become a great

173

friend since we performed together in Basra, he had been giving his services to troop entertainment since 1974; other celebs with whom the BFF had worked in the past include Emma Bunton, Martine McCutcheon, Atomic Kitten and Status Quo. But none of them had been to Basra.

Even before the BFF invitation came, the idea had been in my mind since Dame Vera said to me: 'You must go out and entertain the troops, you know.'

'I will, I will,' I'd promised.

There were, I learned, two ways you could go out and entertain the troops. One is called CSE (Combined Services Entertainment), which is when the government pays entertainers huge amounts of money to go out; the other is when entertainers choose to go out on a voluntary basis, with only their travel and equipment costs met. The latter, I thought, was how it should be, something you take on because you want to do it, not because you're being paid to do it, and I decided I would only do it on a voluntary basis.

When the BFF does the show, its flags are used as a backdrop, which automatically alerts the soldiers to the fact that the artists are doing the show for free. The troops really respect the fact that some entertainers go out there because they want to and not because they are being paid, and they always give these performers a different kind of response. After every trip I did, I always got letters saying how much they appreciated me doing the shows for free. I've heard of some entertainers being paid as much as £80,000 for doing two shows for the troops, and that disgusts me. How they can stand there, earning three times as much in a day as the incredibly brave people they are performing for earn in one year, baffles me. I would never accept a penny.

Having been raised in a part of south Wales that has always been a traditional recruiting ground for the British army, and having had a father who served in the Fleet Air Arm, I feel a great affinity with the troops, and I am also only too aware that several of my young acquaintances from Neath have joined up. So that's how the name 'Forces Sweetheart' came about; and just a few months later, thanks to the BFF, I found myself on a trip to Iraq.

Before then I was whisked off on a visit to troops that included a lot of Royal Welch Fusiliers, stationed near Crossmaglen in Northern Ireland. For this trip, which took place on 19 December 2005 and was, in fact, a training exercise for my visit to Iraq, I went with Jim Davidson, whom I met for the first time at the airport. By then, though, I knew Jim was a legend and that the troops adored him. His humour is so politically incorrect, which, needless to say, goes down very well with the troops, who love his daring.

I'd also been told by Mark Cann, the charity's main organiser and former army officer, that getting me in and out of Basra in a day was going to be BFF's most challenging task yet, hence the training run.

I was nervous, very nervous, but by the time I had finished the trip to Northern Ireland where we travelled around, visiting lots of different people and did a show at the end of the day, I couldn't wait to do more of the same. I sang just about all my songs in Crossmaglen—and as the audience was mostly Welsh they wouldn't let me off stage, but started chanting my name and stamping their feet on the boards.

'I've run out of songs. What can I sing?' I asked, genuinely nonplussed.

'Our song—our song,' they yelled back, meaning, of course, the Welsh national anthem.

'Then you'll have to sing along,' I called back, 'because I don't have a backing track.'

And they did. They all stood up and we belted out an a cappella version. It was all so emotional, so moving. It couldn't have been a better trip for me to get over my fears about the forthcoming visit to Basra, which had been scheduled for 22 December 2005. But, if I had known what a baptism of fire that was going to be, I would not have been feeling so confident.

FIFTEEN

THE FORCES SWEETHEART

Having left for Basra on 22 December 2005, we flew with British Airways from London to Kuwait, and were advised to get as much sleep as we could on the plane because we wouldn't get much, if any, after that. When we touched down in Kuwait, we were taken by jeep straight to the military base, where we got into a huge Sea King helicopter, the type of chopper that has a ramp at the end for loading Land Rovers.

All this was so new for me but, having just come from Northern Ireland, I was so *go-go-go* that when I got on the helicopter and was asked if I would like to sit on the edge of the ramp and look out of the open back, for some silly reason I said, 'Okay'.

The next thing I knew, I had a harness strapped around my waist and I was sitting right on the edge of the ramp. Flying 2,000 feet above the desert, the view is amazing, but when the helicopter is open at the back and there are machine-guns on board it is a trifle unsettling, to say the least.

It was certainly not the kind of thing I would normally do, but as I sat there, completely deafened by the sound of the engine, looking down at the desert, although I felt a bit light-headed and giddy, I was thinking, 'Wow! How bizarre is this,' and I felt really exhilarated. To be honest, I was amazed at myself. Usually I'm terrified of heights and falling; I can't go on rollercoasters for this reason and no amount of money would tempt me to do a bungee jump, yet there I was sitting on the ramp of an in-flight helicopter.

Earlier in the week when I was in Northern Ireland, I had been warned about conditions in Iraq. 'It's very dirty and smelly,' one soldier said, 'and you will need to wash your hands a lot.' Others added: 'It depends on the day. Most of the time it's fine—not so bad really.'

The first scary moment came as we approached the Kuwait/Iraq border. At this point the crew gave us some pre-arranged hand-signals that meant 'the helicopter is now going over the border and you must put on your helmet and flak jacket.' We had been warned, in advance, that crossing the border was the moment when we could get shot down; and, now we were on the approach, it was for me one of those reality-check moments and I felt somewhat nauscous and worried.

'Oh, my gosh,' I found myself thinking, 'what am I doing here? What if . . .' But all went according to plan and we landed safely at the first base right next to the Shatt-al-Arab, where the military had built a camp.

Although there were not many soldiers stationed there at that time, the troops had succeeded in taking over one of Saddam's palaces, which I was taken to see. Much of the palace had been gutted, so there was no furniture, but there was sufficient of the building left intact for it to be used as a headquarters for the UN. Apparently, long before Iraq had been invaded, Saddam had been obsessed with being attacked by insurgents in his own country and, for this reason, his palace had been built surrounded by water on three sides. For this, his workforce had used the natural swampy waterway of Shatt-al-Arab and then constructed two other waterways, so the palace was surrounded by a moat.

It was such a surreal, creepy feeling when I was told I was walking through Saddam's bedroom, and, as I stood on one of its balconies, trying to smile for a photograph that was being taken, I was thinking: 'Never in a thousand years could I have imagined I would ever be standing in Saddam Hussein's bedroom. Perish the thought! And, thank God, he's not here.'

When we went up on the roof, from where we could see the infamous waterways, I was told these were formed by a confluence of the rivers Tigris and Euphrates and that deadly attacks were still a daily occurrence here.

I also began to feel very uneasy when our military escort told us some dark stories about this particular house into which so many political figures had entered, never to be seen again, and where so much torture was known to have taken place. I had often seen news footage at home concerning Saddam's reign of terror, but this felt so real and was, for me, another wake-up call.

The palace itself, when still intact, would have looked like an over the top, gaudy villa with huge high ceilings, enormous rooms, all built on a palatial scale—which, I guess, was right for a palace!

Having finished our visit there, we set off on a boat ride over the dangerous Shatt-al-Arab waterway. On one side of the waterway, we were told, were the British forces and, on the other side, the insurgents who were in the habit of taking pot shots at anything passing by.

I was wearing a flak jacket and padded helmet, and the soldiers were really looking after me, but I was aware that there were still quite a few bits of me that were exposed and could take a sniper's bullet.

One way or another it was really eerie as we sped across as quickly as we could. It was like a graveyard of ships. On several occasions I saw the skeletons of ships lying in the water, ships that had been either abandoned or bombed; as the water was not very deep, the remains of these were still evident, and were constant reminders that we were in a war zone.

A year after I was there, I was very distressed to hear that four British soldiers in a boat on the Shatt-al-Arab were killed by a bomb placed under one of the bridges. When I heard about the incident I had a much better understanding of just how awful it was because I had been there. In fact, whenever I hear about any of our servicemen being killed in Iraq or Afghanistan, I am absolutely gutted and always wonder if I have met or sung to any of them.

Having arrived at Basra Palace, which actually used to be a hotel, we were met in the huge reception hall by lots of different regiments, and had about half an hour to do the rounds and talk to them. They were all such lovely guys and girls. Some gave me T-shirts, some Christmas cards that they had made themselves with messages of thanks to me for coming out.

'Thank you for coming,' one soldier said, 'I never thought I would smile this tour.' Another chap said, 'Welcome to the nightmare, Katherine.' It was a real insight into how some of them were feeling.

From there, we went to the logistics base, where Jim Davidson and I did the first show for 1,500 troops in a massive aircraft hanger: the actual stage was two flat-bed lorries parked back-to-back. Jim's performance was absolutely brilliant and created a great atmosphere. While he was performing, I was waiting in the wings, dressed in a Marc Jacobs dress, which I had deliberately chosen for its patriotic red, white and dark blue stripes. When it came to my turn, and I was singing my heart out on the makeshift stage and trying to keep the tears at bay, I could see the runways where planes and helicopters were constantly taking off and landing.

*   *   *

Oh, yes, helicopters! Having been told this ride was an opportunity to get forty winks before arriving at the next base, I checked my seat belt and harness, which was criss-crossed over my chest and trunk, then felt safe enough to close my eyes for an afternoon nap.

Minutes later, just as I had dozed off, all hell broke loose. To my horror—and, I might add, everybody else's, including the soldiers on board— we heard those urgent words, 'Missile alert at rear!' Not surprisingly, I started screaming. My arms and legs flew into the air from the G-force as the aircraft dropped from 2,000 to 500 feet in a matter of seconds; and the next moment I could see the anti-missile flares going off. We could do nothing but look at each other—and hope and pray we would survive the ground-to-air missile that had been launched at us.

The extraordinary thing about that whole terrifying episode is that, having avoided instant death, I didn't have a moment to think about that when we landed. We literally hit the ground running and, having started at 7 a.m. Iraq time we didn't finish until midnight; we didn't have a minute to ourselves. The entire twelve-hour trip was so frenetic that all I could do was think about what was next, and my second show of the day as a trouper for the troops went ahead as planned.

These days, each time I recall the events of that first day in Iraq, I can't help reminding myself that I was there for only a very short time. Our brave boys and girls, however, face potentially deadly attacks every day. For this reason, if none other, I was determined after that first trip to do more BFF trips in the future.

Having now been several times, I know what to expect. We don't sleep when we are in Iraq. We arrive at seven o'clock in the morning and leave at midnight. Some artists, I learned, sit in their designated room when they are not performing and wait until the show. Not me. When I go, I want to maximise my time and see as many of the troops as I can, so I get taken around all the areas on what is usually called a 'meet and greet', but what the military call a 'grip and grin'.

For obvious reasons, I always hope the performances will bring some light relief and good cheer to the troops and that my singing will touch their hearts; but I am sure that what they most want to do is talk to somebody from home, and I try to spend as much time as possible with them. This, however, often only amounts to about two minutes with each of them, asking how they are coping, when they were last home, when they are next on leave; and, if they're Welsh, I chat about the rugby. Those moments for me are even more important than singing them a few songs.

We all think we know what it's like out there because we watch some of the footage on TV, but it isn't until you see the conditions in which our soldiers are living and working that you realise it takes really special people to do this work. It was such a privilege to spend time with them; each time I go, I am left with nothing but admiration for them. To see the conditions under which they work helped me to appreciate what is asked of them on our behalf. It's not something I will ever forget. There's a real sense of strength and togetherness, of camaraderie, and I felt so proud to be a part of it.

The next base we flew to for a 'meet and greet' after the missile attack was home to an Irish regiment, and the Irish, bless them, put on a very high-spirited concert for us in the mess, which consisted entirely of Irish-Celtic music. Once this was under way, they got Jim and me up on to the stage to sing and play percussion, which was tremendous fun. From there, we were due to move on to the last base where the second gig was to be held; and just as we walked towards the departure area expecting a brief wait and a cup of tea, we were led towards an enormous vehicle—the largest I had ever seen.

'What's that for?' I asked.

'It's a tank transporter,' I was told.

It was shaped like a gigantic lorry, but could carry three tanks.

'Are we going in that?' I gasped.

'Yes, we're going to drive it to the next place. But would you like to drive, Kath?'

The offer was irresistible.

'Can I?'

As there were two of these transporters, Jim climbed into one and I went in the other, with an instructor seated alongside me in the passenger seat, who showed me how to brake, steer and accelerate, while he leaned over and changed the gears.

There were, I soon discovered, a lot of checkpoints on that base, which meant I had to manoeuvre the tank very carefully to get it through the gates. I managed the first one really well, so well I started to enjoy gazing all around me. Then, arriving at our destination, I drove the tank through the final checkpoint and parked it. I was so proud of myself as I jumped down from the driver's seat.

'Well done, Katherine,' my driving instructor said. 'I've never known anyone to be as good as you on their first time in the driving seat.'

Swelling with pride, I went straight over to Jim and said, 'Hey, Jim, before you make any jokes about women drivers, did you see my driving? How *fab-lous* was that?'

'Are you joking, Katherine?' he replied, chortling. 'I just saw you knock a wall down on the way in.'

I thought he was winding me up, but when I went to look I discovered it was true. Apparently as I went through the checkpoint, the back of the vehicle had knocked down the wall, and it was now a pile of rubble.

'Oh, gosh,' I said to one of the officers, 'I'm

sorry, I've just knocked down your wall.'

'Don't worry, Katherine,' he replied cheerfully, 'we'll just rebuild it.'

I crept away, mortified.

I really didn't know how my music would go down and I suspected a lot of them, possibly the majority, had never really listened to classical music. Anyway, I tried to choose songs that they would at least know the tunes of; and at the two short performances I gave—the first in a giant hangar at the airport and a later one in the evening at Shaibah—I offered them a sample menu of my crossover songs, such as operatic aria-turned-footie-anthem 'Nessun Dorma', 'Over the Rainbow', and my version of Dolly Parton's 'I Will Always Love You'. I then ended with another football favourite, 'You'll Never Walk Alonc', because the words are so appropriate to express what I wanted to convey to them: that we were all there for them and proud of what they were trying to achieve.

I must say, even though there wasn't the faintest trace of an electric guitar in my pre-recorded back-up tracks that I sang to, the soldiers listened with rapt attention while I was singing and applauded very warmly at the end.

The second of the shows, which was really an open-air concert for about four thousand troops, went down exceptionally well, which is always a great relief. What really took me by surprise was that when I was singing 'Over the Rainbow', all the troops sang it with me. It was such an emotional moment. I could see some of them gazing up at me through tear-filled eyes. I usually get very upset when I am singing my last song but, that time, I was

185

completely overwhelmed.

'I hope this will not sound patronising,' I said, my voice almost stifled by emotion, 'but I want you to know that everybody at home is thinking of you this Christmas and so proud of you.'

The bit that really got to me on that first occasion, though—and every time since—is when I added, 'Stay safe', because nobody knows how many of them will stay safe.

When I came off stage and went to the dressing-room area at the end of the second show, some of the soldiers presented me with my own set of desert combats. I was so touched I burst into tears. It was a lovely gift. I'd been admiring their combats all day, because they're such lovely colours—Jim had nicknamed me 'GI Jenkins' on that trip—and they'd embroidered Jenkins on the shirt pocket in the exact place where they have their surnames, which was so thoughtful.

When I got the chance to speak to a couple more of the soldiers before we left, one of them said to me: 'Think of us when you're having your Christmas dinner, Katherine. We won't be getting a very nice one here.'

'I will . . . I promise I will,' I replied, grasping him by the hand.

Then we took the helicopter back to the air base, followed by a flight to Kuwait, where we had a little time to rest in a hotel before catching our plane to London.

Once in the hotel at Kuwait, I called my mum and said, 'Just in case you hear it on the news, Mum, we did get fired at but we are fine.'

'Oh, my God . . . you're never going there again,' Mum said, freaking out.

'But I am, Mum.'

Then I called Steve who was at our friend Sophie's house.

'Thank God you're safe,' he said, as Sophie burst into tears and kept repeating, 'I'm gonna kill them . . . I'm gonna kill them . . .'

Sophie really was hysterical; and, ever since then, when I go off on a BFF trip, she throws holy water over me, which she gets from Lourdes; and, because she's my beautician as well as my friend, she insists on putting holy water into a specially made up pot of my aromatherapy oils.

'Keep using this,' she tells me. 'It will keep you safe.'

Having had a couple of hours of much needed sleep in Kuwait, I boarded the plane for London. The trip had been so action-packed, I was still well and truly wound up. I'd met so many wonderful people, but there had been hardly any time to absorb everything that had happened.

It's hard to explain, but when you are out there with the troops you feel part of a huge family—and I find military people so well-mannered, so disciplined, and I love the way everyone calls you Ma'am! Yes, parts of the trip had been terrifying, but I just kept thinking, 'Wow! How lucky was I to be able to witness and be part of all that.' It really was incredible.

When I arrived back in London at about two o'clock in the afternoon on Christmas Eve, I collected my car and drove down the M4 to Neath, getting there at about six in the evening, just as there was an item mentioning I had been in Iraq on the television news.

Every Christmas Eve, Laura and I go into town

187

for a few drinks, always at the same pub, then go on to Midnight Mass. It all felt so surreal. As I walked into the pub, everyone looked up astonished and said, 'But you're in Iraq.'

'I was, earlier today,' I replied.

Then, there in the middle of Neath, my mobile rang and it was Jim Davidson, who had just got back home. You really form a strong bond when you share an experience like the one we had just shared, and it was so lovely to talk to each other, especially as he insisted on singing a variation of a well-known Christmas song to me over the telephone:

And so this is Christmas,
And what have we done?
A missile just missed us,
Isn't life fun!

As the call came to an end, everything—all my surroundings, complete with Christmas tree and lights, and the people dancing and making merry— suddenly seemed unreal. Everything was so familiar and normal, but I had just come back from a war zone where I'd nearly been shot down in a helicopter, and I hadn't yet made the readjustment and didn't feel a part of the scene I now found myself in. After a while these feelings began to wear off, but while they lasted I felt curiously detached and everything felt very strange.

The next day while I was eating my Christmas dinner, I felt very shaky and sick, and I realised I was only just beginning to absorb the shock of the whole experience; and, for a week after that, I had terrifying flashbacks and nightmares every night. I

Singing at the Royal Variety Performance at the Millennium Centre, Cardiff, November 2005, and below, meeting the Queen afterwards. (Ken McKay/Rex Features)

Having fun appearing on the catwalk for Naomi Campbell's Fashion For Relief show, held as part of London Fashion Week, to raise money for the Rotary Flood Disaster Appeal. (David Fisher/Rex Features)

eceiving an honorary fellowship from the Royal Welsh College of
Music and Drama, Cardiff, in July 2006. My singing teacher
eatrice Unsworth was also made an honorary fellow. (Huw
ohn/Rex Features)

Dame Kiri and I in the studio
recording a track together for
Serenade.

Me and Steve on holiday.

Wearing a dress made up of 2,500 poppies as I joined forces with The Royal British Legion to officially launch the 2006 Poppy Appeal, in Covent Garden, London. (PA Photos)

Appearing on 'Parky', 23 December 2006, with Dame Judi Dench and Lenny Henry (Ken McKay/Rex Features), and below, meeting Parky afterwards with the family.

Above My sister Laura, Kristy and me on holiday in Spain, 2006.

Left One of the highlights of my career so far—singing with Placido Domingo, in Athens, June 2007. (Dimitrios Legakis)

Showing off my new
Wellington boots at the
Katherine in the Park event
in the grounds of Margam
Park in South Wales, July
2007 and below, singing with
Paul Potts on the night.
(PA Photos)

In a boat travelling up the Shat al Arab in Basra.

In Iraq 2005, just after the helicopter missile incident. not looking too happy, am I

With Goose.

Iraq 2005.

Jim Davidson,
me and the
troops at Basra
Palace, 2005.

Lunch in
Afghanistan.

VE Day 60th Anniversary 'Party to Remember' concert at Trafalgar Square. (PA Photos)

Singing 'We'll Meet Again' to Vera Lynn on her 90th birthday at the Imperial War Museum, London, in March 2007. (Stephen Lock/Rex Features)

Arriving at the Classical Brit Awards 2007 with Juan Diego Florez, and below, singing later on.
(Rex Features)

Left Meeting Prince Charles at Salisbury Cathedral in November 2007, celebrating 50 years of the Army Air Corps.

Viva La Diva, a show I'm doing with ballerina Darcey Bussell, which combines dance and music. I'm actually doing some dancing myself, so I'm right out of my comfort zone! (Iris Brosch)

kept thinking I was back, flying over the desert in Basra; or thinking: 'If I was at home, why were the troops not at home, too?' I felt really guilty that I had gone out there for only a couple of days and they were there for six months. That really bothered me and played on my conscience. So, in January, when I received an invitation from Jim to become a Trustee of the British Forces Foundation, I knew immediately that this was something I wanted to do; that my visit to Iraq wasn't a one-off; that I wanted to be involved with the BFF for the long haul, and take part in the decision-making processes for fund-raising to encourage top-class performers to go around the world entertaining our troops. In fact, on my way back in the plane from Kuwait I had actually said to Jim, clapping my hands, 'Right, Jim, where are we going next?'

And he's made it my catchphrase: 'Right, Jim,' he'd say, smiling and imitating my Welsh lilt, 'where are we going next?'

SIXTEEN

BREAKING RECORDS

'Sweetie, how do you like your bodyguards?'

I guess, by now, I should have been getting used to peculiar questions like that when I was borrowing jewellery, but thinking the guy was joking, I replied, 'Oh, make him as gorgeous as you can.'

'Right. What do you fancy: an ex-policeman, ex-fireman, ex-marine?'

'Oh,' I said, going with the flow, 'an ex-marine would do nicely, thank you. Yes, I could definitely cope with an ex-marine bodyguard.'

This chit-chat had come about because I was borrowing some jewellery for the Classical BRIT Awards, which were being hosted by Michael Parkinson and taking place on 4 May 2007. Once inside the shop, I had ended up choosing about £200,000 worth of diamond-encrusted earrings, a ring and two bracelets.

'You will look *gor-geous* in those,' the guy in charge had said, in a sweet attempt to imitate my pronunciation of 'gorgeous', 'but, of course, you will have to have a bodyguard for the jewellery.' I had expected that, but had genuinely thought he was joking about what kind of bodyguard I fancied. He was not.

For the BRITs, we always get ready at the Royal Garden Hotel, Kensington, which is close to the Albert Hall. On this occasion, I was presenting the Contemporary Music Award to James Macmillan and had been nominated for the Album of the Year Award for *Living A Dream*. This meant I was not actually performing and could, therefore, really enjoy most of the evening without having to worry about being in good voice. I could just sit there at the table, eat my dinner and take everything in until it was time for me to make the presentation.

So, there I was at the Royal Garden Hotel with my hair and make-up team, starting to get ready, when there was a knock on the door; and when I went to answer it, there was this *gor-geous* man, and, as I looked at him, my jaw dropped almost to the floor and I burst out laughing.

He must have thought, 'How rude', but he just said, 'I'm Jamie, Miss Jenkins. I'm here to look after you and the jewellery tonight.'

Trying to recover my composure, I replied, 'Well, Jamie, I'm going to be a couple of hours. Why don't you keep the jewellery for the moment and go to the bar, and we'll call you when we are ready.' When I closed the door, the girls and I just went to pieces, cracking up, because, although I had told them the story of my visit to the shop, none of us had expected this handsome ex-marine to turn up.

Later that day, when we were travelling by limo to do the red carpet bit at the Albert Hall, I turned to Jamie who was sitting alongside me.

'Jamie,' I said, 'I must apologise.'

Then I told him the story behind my strange behaviour, adding, 'I asked, but I honestly didn't expect to get such a *gor-geous* ex-marine and, when I opened the door, there you were. So, please, don't think I was laughing at you.'

Earlier in the year I had watched the 1953 film

How To Marry A Millionaire in which my adored Marilyn Monroe wore an amazing dress in a magenta colour.

'Yes!' I exclaimed. 'That's it. That's what I want to wear for this year's BRIT.'

I didn't want my dress to be just an exact copy, though. I wanted a re-designed younger version of it. So I decided to have it made in bright fuchsia pink and encrusted in sparkling gems. Later on, of course, the tabloids wrote that the dress, made by my fabulous dressmakers, the Kruszynska sisters, cost £75,000. There was only one problem with that fab dress on the night. As it was very slinky and corseted, this meant when I was presenting the award to the composer/conductor James Macmillan I could hardly breathe.

The mega excitement of the day, however, was that my *Living A Dream* album had been nominated for the Album of the Year award. As I had been lucky enough to win this award the previous year for *Second Nature*, I was convinced there was no way they were going to let me win it twice in a row. So sure was I that I couldn't possibly win a Classical BRIT Award two years running that I hadn't even written a just-in-case thank-you speech.

So, there I was, just sitting at the table with my mum, Steve and Brian and the Universal execs, with Jamie waving at me every now and again. Then, as I listened to the nominations and album titles, including 'Katherine Jenkins—*Living A Dream*', being read out, the Taffia (my aunties, cousins, friends and neighbours) let out a huge scream and started waving the massive banner they'd made, which said, 'We love you Kath'; and, once again as in the previous year, I started having palpitations and thought I was going to stop breathing. Apart from anything else, the corseted dress was not helping matters. Then, unbelievably, I heard the words 'The winner is . . . Katherine Jenkins—*Living A Dream*', and I just thought, 'No! Oh, my God, that's just not possible' and, as I looked at Mum's face and realised it was true, I burst into tears. My next thought, as I struggled to my feet to make the long walk to the stage was, 'O-h-h-h-h, my God, I haven't prepared a speech.'

The Album of the Year Award at the BRITs is the award that means the most to me as it is the one that is voted for by the public—and such moments can take an age to sink in. Hardly able to breathe, suffering dreadful palpitations and still crying, I was a real mess by the time I got up on the stage. To make matters worse, speaking in public was a bugbear I hadn't yet mastered. I enjoyed speaking to audiences as I do in my shows, but if I have to get up and give a speech, like the one at the BRITs, I'm absolutely terrified.

On this occasion, having somehow managed to thank everyone, I said, 'I honestly never thought that I would win this one. Once again, my dad's not here, but this one, the second one, is for my dad, too.'

As I came off stage to make my way towards the waiting press, Placido Domingo was standing in the wings, waiting to go up to get his Lifetime Achievement Award. That moment, when Placido and I exchanged words, was the start of our friendship; and that moment, coming off stage with my award and meeting Placido, remains one of my best memories of that night. We had a lovely chat and he invited me to go and watch his rehearsals at Covent Garden Opera House the following morning.

The next day I read some reviews of the Classical BRIT awards in which people were saying they couldn't believe I didn't know that I had won; that I was obviously an extremely good actress, but I certainly wouldn't have succeeded in crying my eyes out at the table if I had known in advance I was the winner and I wouldn't have been able to look so shocked. So, what they were writing really upset me because I wasn't acting up for the cameras. It was a genuine reaction.

The one person who had known all day that I was going to win was Jamie, because, as my bodyguard, he had to know exactly where I was going to be at all times, and also had to plan a quick escape route for us. I also suspect that the record company execs and Brian knew. But I didn't. I do realise that if I had looked at the sales figures for my *Living A Dream* album at that time, I might have thought to myself, 'Maybe I will win,' but I didn't.

Other journalists just kept to the facts and told their readers that, aged twenty-five, I had 'beaten off competition from Welsh operatic baritone Bryn Terfel, violinist Nicola Benedetti and ex-*Emmerdale* actress Amy Nuttall, and scooped Album of the Year at the Classical BRIT Awards for the second year running; and had brought Hollywood glamour along with my £75,000 fuchsia pink dress, which was set off by £250,000 worth of diamonds.'

That night in the press room, I tried my best to talk to everybody who wanted to speak to me. This is important because it's the one day of the year when you get a chance to acknowledge in public all the people you work with, all the really generous, talented guys and girls who help to make things happen.

Afterwards, I took all my family, friends and colleagues to the celebratory party that Universal Classics had arranged at The Volt, near Buckingham Palace. The party was descended upon by my family and the entire Taffia. Everyone who knows me knows and loves the Taffia and appreciates that this is the one occasion in the year when I can really let my hair down.

At some point during these evenings, we always sing our family song, which, most appropriately, is the Sister Sledge number, 'We are Family'. My mum has two sisters and I have lots of cousins and I cannot think of a better song for us. My abiding memories of these occasions is having a few glasses of champagne, then joining the Taffia in a massive circle and singing 'We are famil-eeeeee', while still clutching my BRIT. That's an absolutely wonderful, memorable moment in my life.

Jamie, my bodyguard, was very much in demand that night. He was so handsome all my family and the Taffia wanted to meet him—and, as he obviously had to stay close to my side to keep an eye on the jewellery, they did. I even had to tell him when I was going to the toilet; and, at one point, I said, 'Oh, Jamie, I want to go and dance. Will you hold this for me?' So, there he stood for the rest of the party, holding my jewel-encrusted handbag in one hand and my Classical BRIT Award in the other, while still keeping an eye on me.

I had broken a record that night, I was told, by

becoming the first female artist ever to win two consecutive classical BRIT awards for Best Album. It was another perfect day.

'This can't keep happening. I won't be nominated for an award next year,' I warned the Taffia, who were already looking forward to cheering me on again. 'There's no way I can be nominated three years running.'

'Bet you will,' they kept replying.

Needless to say, having let my hair down at the BRIT party, I was not feeling my best the next day, but I still got out of bed early to go and see Placido Domingo in rehearsal for *Cyrano de Bergerac*.

After the rehearsal, I went backstage to say 'Hi' to him, which confirmed once again what a lovely, charismatic man he is. Often when you meet people who are huge stars, they are completely different off-stage or off-camera. But not Placido. When he comes off stage, he speaks to every single person with the same degree of respect, the same grace and manners, which is something I love to see. He is such a legend and yet he is such a nice, generous person.

A few days later, I could hardly believe it when he called and invited me to go to the performance of *Cyrano de Bergerac* and then to have dinner with him afterwards. When I did, I found him to be a total inspiration. He is so open, so ready to share his experiences, and he gave me lots of advice for when I am ready to enter the world of opera. Quite simply, he is a gentleman and one of the nicest people I have ever met.

*   *   *

'We'd like you to be our ambassador,' Wolff Heinrichsdorff and Lutz Bethge, the CEOs at Montblanc, the German luxury goods company based in Hamburg, said.

Apparently some of their people had heard me sing at Live 8 in Berlin and, when I was invited to a meeting with the UK side of the company in the spring of 2006, I also received an invitation to go to Hamburg to visit them at their headquarters and do a tour of the factory, which produces the beautiful pens they are so famous for.

Brian and I went to meet them and they invited me to be their brand ambassador, in particular, for their new female range of fine jewellery.

I'd had lots of previous requests to do endorsements and work with companies, but I'd never been interested in doing that kind of thing until Montblanc came along. I'd always thought their brand, which is elegant and feminine, was exactly the sort of thing I would want to buy; and, as I like to think I'm ladylike and elegant, it was a perfect brand for me to represent.

I was also impressed by the fact that Montblanc is a company that really encourages culture and the arts. They constantly commission new pieces of artwork; and, four times a year, they invite a symphony orchestra to come to their factory in Hamburg to play for the workers.

Now that I'm their brand ambassador, I have my own set of all the jewellery they make and get to keep it. How *lovely* is that! It has also been very interesting to see how they do things. I'd done some modelling in the past, but this was completely different and on such a vast scale. Every time we go to a new city these days, there are enormous billboards of me wearing Montblanc jewellery.

The first time I saw a truly large billboard was on my first visit to Tokyo when, accompanied by Montblanc's Wolff Heinrichsdorff, I went to cut a ribbon to open a new Montblanc flagship store in Ginza district. As I got out of the car, there on either side of the shop entrance were enormous six-foot-high pictures of me.

'That looks amazing, Wolff,' I said.

'You haven't seen anything yet,' he replied, laughing, as he walked me round to the side of the building; and there, going up the entire side of this eleven-storey-high skyscraper was my picture. I was stunned, and just couldn't stop staring at it, my jaw on the ground. Then, as I turned round to look at Brian to say, 'Do you believe this, Brian?' I noticed that a crowd of Japanese people had gathered and were taking photographs of me looking at my billboard.

In many different ways, being an ambassador has been really good fun; and because there are so many photo opportunities and I meet so many people, I always keep my camera in my bag, so that I can take my own pics and email them to my family.

'This is the new billboard,' I say. 'Can you believe it?'

SEVENTEEN

TIME TO SAY GOODBYE

It is a moment all performers dread; a moment when their private and professional worlds collide. Inevitably, given 'the show must go on' tradition in show business, it is usually our public who must come first. Coming as I do, though, from a place where the most important things are to stay grounded and to keep your family around you, I found that a very hard tradition to take on board; and I still get distraught when I think about the two tragic personal events that collided with my career at the end of summer 2006.

My nanna, who was ninety years old, had been ill for over a year, but while I was on a tour in Japan, worrying about her, Mum called me with some other distressing news about another member of our family. My Auntie Betty—my great aunt, sister of Nanna's husband—had died. We were very close to her, so that was upsetting enough, but Mum also told me that Nanna had been taken very ill and wasn't expected to live.

I was devastated and wanted to leave Japan at once; but I was told that if I went home I would probably never work in Japan again. The culture there is that nothing interferes with business. I had never ever cancelled a concert and certainly didn't want to let down the organisers of my concerts, but it was a really tough decision. In the end, though, Nanna's health improved slightly and I was able to proceed with the tour.

211

Just a few months later when I was in London, Mum called and told me that Nanna had taken a turn for the worse again and, as we all wanted the inevitable to happen at home, the medical people had put a hospital bed in her own house, just eleven doors down from ours. So, having received the news I'd been dreading for some time, I jumped into my car, dashed down to Wales, and sat by Nanna's bedside. I was actually due to go on a BFF trip to Kosovo for two days to entertain the troops in September 2006, but I stayed with her until the last possible second, then went straight to the airport.

To be honest, I hardly remember anything about those two days in Kosovo, because, all the time I was there, I was expecting a phone call from Mum to say that the worst had happened. On that trip, I went with Jim Davidson and the singer-songwriter James Blunt who, when he was serving as a reconnaissance officer in the army in 1990, was the first British officer to go into Pristina. During his time in Kosovo, he also wrote his song, 'No Bravery', while lying in a sleeping bag in his tank with his boots still on.

Our audience, while we were there, was a mix of British troops and some Kosovans and, despite my anxieties and sense of dread, I could still appreciate the great atmosphere that greeted us there. Miraculously, Mum's call didn't come, so when I got back to the UK I was able to dash back to Neath again and spend the next two days at Nanna's bedside.

She really was very poorly and sleeping a great deal, but I was able to tell her I was going away on tour to Australia soon and I felt she understood.

212

She had always let me know how proud she was of me and now, when it was a struggle for her to speak, I got the impression that she was trying to say she didn't want to interrupt what I had to do.

Mum and I sat with her and as I had just finished recording my fourth album, *Serenade*, I played it to her. 'Dear Lord and Father of Mankind' was her favourite hymn and I had included this especially for her on my new disc. When that one came on, Mum and I started to sing along to it, but we quickly lost our composure and fell apart. I think it will be a long time before I can sing that live.

It was heartbreaking: I knew when I left to go to Australia for just over three weeks I wouldn't see her again, and I was absolutely devastated when I was saying goodbye. The moment I touched down in Perth and got to my hotel room, I called home.

'You must be psychic,' Mum said, her voice breaking. 'Nanna's just this moment passed away.'

Since then I've always believed in the 'mind over matter theory': that people can hold on as long as they need to—and I am sure that Nanna waited until I arrived in Australia when she knew it would be impossible for me to turn back. Had she died when I was on my way to the airport, I wouldn't have gone and, knowing that, she waited until I was on the other side of the world.

Mum and I talked on the phone about the funeral and decided that I should stay in Australia and fulfil my contracts there. Again it was a very tough decision, especially as the funeral would be taking place while I was on stage at the State Theatre, Sydney. Not surprisingly, this proved to be one of the hardest shows I have ever had to do. I managed somehow to get through the concert, but

Nanna's death and funeral was on my mind all the time. Then, as I felt I didn't want the moment to pass without saying anything, when I came back on stage for the encore, I said to the audience, 'Somebody very, very dear to me has passed away and I want to dedicate the next song, "My Way", which is so appropriate to that person's life, to her.' I choked over some of the words and couldn't see the audience through my tears, but I managed to hold myself together until I left the stage. Once back in my dressing room, however, I sobbed my heart out, then, having composed myself, called home to see how things were there.

People don't realise—how can they?—that there are times when you are on stage performing when there are distressing things going on in your life. I'm lucky that my mum has always been such a strong role model, and that's what keeps me grounded and stops me falling apart. I know if I did crack up, though, that Mum and Laura and the rest of the family would be there as fast as their feet could carry them, as I would be for them. And it's that knowledge that gives me the strength to go on sometimes without them at my side. Seeing how strong Mum was, how she coped with Dad and everything that happened while I was growing up, has made it possible for me to say to myself: 'I will get through this', followed by 'it's what Dad and Nanna would have wanted. What they would have expected of me.' But it's so hard at times.

I was thrilled, though, while thinking of Dad and Nanna, two of the most important and influential people in my life, to be asked to kick off the 2006 rugby Autumn internationals by recording my new single, 'Green Green Grass of Home' with 74,000

214

rugby supporters as my backing singers. Then, just before Wales took on Australia, I performed that song again, knowing that for every single sold, Universal Classics had pledged to donate thirty pence to Macmillan Cancer Support.

I was equally delighted to launch the 2006 Royal British Legion Poppy Appeal in Covent Garden's Piazza, wearing a dress made of 2,500 poppies, to signal the start of a massive well-deserved fund-raising appeal.

I have learned that, at times when tragedy strikes one's life, there is no greater solace than being able to honour the memory of loved ones by using your talents to give something back to others. And that's what I try to do.

*   *   *

Around about that time, the pressures of work were certainly building up and getting to me, especially during the September to Christmas period, when I often had only four to five hours sleep a night, and didn't get to see any of my friends. There were, and are, times when I find this quite testing, but somehow I get through it. The pressures themselves stem mainly from feeling exhausted, while still having to worry about the need to look and sound good. I want to do everything perfectly, but sometimes there are just not enough hours in the day to succeed in this.

For example, in the early days after I had sung the anthem at the rugby matches, I was able to slip into a seat in the stands, but that ceased to be a good idea once my face became more and widely recognised. At half time, one person would come over to greet me and, within seconds, I'd be surrounded by people, which could at times become quite scary when I found myself in the middle of 200 or so rugby supporters, and everywhere I turned somebody would be asking for an autograph or to be photographed with me. Everyone is lovely but because I'm not very tall, I can't see over the heads of people, so I'm easily overwhelmed and quickly begin to feel claustrophobic and panic-stricken. At one international game there was a particularly scary incident when a guy suddenly leaned over the side of a stand and started to lick my hair. He just grabbed a clump, held on and licked it. Fortunately someone rescued me immediately.

Most of my so-called free time, though, is usually spent helping my body to recover from the rigours of a concert or a tour, so I work out at the gym, rest and relax, or do something quiet with my girlfriends. I love going to the opera when I can, but, more and more often these days, I like to spend time at home. If I do have a whole spare day, I always want to see my mum, so I drive to Neath.

By November 2006, then, when I was twenty-six years old, I had discovered that living a dream had its sacrifices and down side, but it was still my dream, still something I would not have missed, or changed, for the world.

It's just as well I still felt that way because something was about to happen between Steve and me that would leave me completely devastated.

*　　　*　　　*

I have only been in love twice in my life, once with

Kevin, then with Steve. By 2006 I had been with Steve for five and a half years. Halfway through our relationship, my life had changed beyond all recognition, and I went from being around all the time while I was a student at the Royal Academy of Music, and then a teacher, to never being there at all. Once I signed my record deal I led a bird-of-passage existence.

The fact that Steve was a successful singer himself did help; he understood the pressures of the business I was in and accepted that I had to go on tour for weeks on end, but it's hard to sustain a close, passionate relationship when you're so rarely in the same country. Long-distance relationships can, I think, work for some people in some situations for some of the time, and ours did for quite a long time, but you can't live like that forever. The worst thing is when you are in a completely different time zone, which means when you call your partner in your morning, they are either about to go to bed or are in bed. For obvious reasons, you are out of sync with each other and you can end up not really being able to communicate.

I still adored Steve, always knew we would remain the best of friends, but I knew we had grown apart and were not communicating in the same way. In the end, there was no big argument or ugly scene in which we decided we never wanted to see each other again. We just talked things over and decided—and it was a mutual decision—that it was no longer the right time for us; that we couldn't go on as we were and we should therefore separate, but stay in touch and see what happened. As a passionate, all-or-nothing person, who can never say 'never', I found this the least painful way for us to bring our relationship to an end.

It has always been really important for me to have the independence to further my career, but with Steve I had also enjoyed having someone really special in my life; someone to whom I could tell everything and know he was always there for me.

As he knew the business I am in so well, he'd always given me such good advice when I needed it; he had warned me about artists getting carried away, becoming too self-centred, and, from day one, I was determined that would not happen to me, that no amount of success would change me.

Through Steve's example, I also learned how important it is to be in charge of what I'm doing, to take responsibility, and not to be tempted to leave everything to others to sort out. These days, for example, every decision comes through me and, from time to time, I still make a point of checking that things are being done properly.

Steve has a very charismatic personality and has a great way with everyone. He's just one of those people who can enter a room and, with one sentence, have everybody laughing. I'd always admired that so much in him, and always thought that being with him was a wonderful opportunity to listen, watch and learn from somebody with that special kind of gift and talent.

After we split, I kept all his advice in mind, especially the best-ever piece of advice that he gave me, which was: 'Don't ever believe your own hype'—and I never have.

Steve was my world for five and a half years, a world that we had shared with Mister, our miniature Jack Russell, whom we both adored, but when we parted, given the nature of my work and the life I lead, we had to decide that Mister should remain with Steve when I moved out.

After we broke up, the immediate aftermath was painful, stressful and lonely. I *missed* him so much—missed him as my friend. But I still knew we had done the right thing.

It wasn't until I read something that the journalist, Christine Hines, had written in *Hello* magazine a few months later that I began to understand a little better why Steve and I had broken up.

Christine, who has done several interviews with me and who has, therefore, gained a fair idea of what I am about, wrote in her article that I am a 100 per cent person who has to do everything 100 per cent—and the fact that I couldn't give 100 per cent to my relationship with Steve because my work schedule was so intense, just broke me in half. When I read this, I knew it was true; knew that was exactly how I felt; knew that was why I was so unhappy.

It really is a fact of life that if I can't do something perfectly, it tears me apart. For example, if I'm ever going to be a stay-at-home mum and a housewife, I want to make sure I'm going to be the best ever. And, likewise, there is no way right now I can do what I do and be anybody's girlfriend and be good at it.

However, having said that, I remain a 'never say never' girl who is a firm believer in fate intervening. We never know what's around the next corner, do we, and in a few years' time I may feel completely differently. Who knows? As John Lennon once

said, and it has proved to be true time and time
again, 'Life is what happens when you are making
other plans!'

EIGHTEEN

BITTER-SWEET SMELL OF SUCCESS

I'd had so many triumphs in such a short time but was feeling the loss of Steve very acutely. I had plenty on my mind, not least a sell-out concert tour of Australia and the Far East, and my new album, which we had decided to call *Serenade*. I noticed when listening to *Serenade* that my voice had changed, that it had settled slightly. It wasn't that my bottom range had grown; it was more that my voice felt more natural and comfortable, a little lower than it had been before.

Interviewers kept asking me: 'What made you decide to do a version of the Bryan Adams' song "(Everything I Do) I Do It For You" on your latest album *Serenade,* and what was he like to work with?'

'I really enjoyed picking that song and giving it a classical treatment,' I replied. 'When I was about to record, I thought of songs that I loved and had been important to me—and the Bryan Adams' track was one of them.'

When I mentioned this to Brian, my manager, he was his usual cheeky self and asked Bryan Adams if he would play guitar on my new album; and Bryan, bless him, said yes. Then, as I had also seen some of Bryan's fabulous photos, I also decided to ask him if he would shoot my album cover. I am so pleased he agreed because I think he did an amazing job. Both the guitar playing and the photographs were great.

221

As well as that song, I sang a selection of arias, pop and traditional songs, and hymns, including 'Green, Green Grass of Home', 'The Prayer', 'Ave Maria', 'Chanson Bohème' from Bizet's *Carmen* and Puccini's 'O Mio Babbino Caro'.

On one of the tracks, I had the great honour of partnering Dame Kiri Te Kanawa in Delibes's 'The Flower Duet', which was very special because I'd always wanted to record that duet—one that, for as long as I could remember, I was always singing. For example, whenever it was party time with my family or friends, it was the 'The Flower Duet' that Laura Thomas, a friend from my church choir days, and I were always asked to sing. I guess you could call it our party piece.

Anyway, by the time I was making *Serenade* and was in a position to ask for a leading artist to be involved in the album, I decided to start with my first choice, Dame Kiri, whom I've always admired and had seen in recent times performing at the BRITs. I was thrilled when I heard that she had agreed.

When she came into the studio, I was really nervous about meeting somebody I had so admired for such a long time, but she was lovely and immediately put me at my ease. Although she had a terrible cold and was very snuffly, she was so professional.

'Don't worry,' she said, 'I'll be fine.'

And she was. Within a couple of takes, she was done and had performed it perfectly. A couple of days after that I woke up to find I had a cold—but as it was pretty certain to be Dame Kiri's, I thought it was a very special cold, so I forgave her!

Like my other albums, I dedicated *Serenade* to

my dad, Selwyn; but this time I added: 'I would also like to dedicate it in memory of my beloved Nanna, who sadly passed away during the making of this record, and to everyone who took such good care of her.'

Serenade, Brian told me, had entered the charts at number one in the classical charts, number five in the pop charts and sold more than 50,000 copies in its first week, making it 'the fastest-selling classical CD in Britain'. 'It'll certainly be a double platinum,' he added. That was a moment when I felt as if I'd jumped over the moon.

The 'Taffia'—Mum, Laura, Gavin, Jo, Alan, Naomi, Hannah, Ruth, Louise, Cyril, Melanie, Jason, Jakob, Gavin, Olivia, Kelly, Chris, Jeanne, Grifydd and Denzil, couldn't have been more excited and supportive, and kept telling me *Serenade* would certainly be nominated for 'Album of the Year' at the BRITs, and that they were saving their biggest cheer ever for that occasion. With those words ringing in my ears, I set off on a sell-out twenty-seven-date UK tour to promote the new album.

*   *   *

At the beginning of December 2006, I went to Iraq again, and this time the weather was completely different. On my first visit it had been T-shirt weather, really hot and sunny, but this time it was cold, foggy, uncomfortable and much harder physically and emotionally because the morale of the troops was so much lower. On this occasion I flew out with a camera crew from ITV, Gary Rhodes, the chef, and the comedian Joe Pasquale, who had recently been the winner of the TV show *I'm a Celebrity Get Me Out of Here*. As Jim Davidson wasn't on this trip, I took over his role of encouraging everyone and explaining everything they needed to know.

We did two shows that went down really well, then I was asked to go and present some special Christmas gifts to certain members of the troops. One of these was to a soldier from his wife, and the gift was a DVD that showed the scan of the baby she was carrying, their first baby. As I showed it to him, he was so overwhelmed by the sheer emotion of seeing his unborn child he burst into tears, and I cried with him. 'He's going home for the first time for the birth,' I was told, 'will stay a week, then come back again to Iraq.'

After each show I continued to go out into the crowd to 'grip and greet' as many of them as possible. That remained more important for me than actually singing to them; and the more I did it, the more I knew what to ask and what to talk about. On one occasion when I was surrounded by several hundred of the military, I noticed a young soldier, the youngest I had ever seen, trying to get my attention. And this turned out to be one of those unexpected, heart-melting moments.

'How are you?' I asked.

'I don't want to be here, Katherine,' he said, tears welling up in his eyes. 'I just want to go home.'

'Listen,' I said, taking hold of his hand, 'when do you go home next?'

'Not for ages. I've only been here five weeks and I *hate* it. I don't want to be here.'

That encounter broke my heart. I wanted to take

him home with me and cuddle him. He had opened up his heart to me because there was nobody else he could say those things to, and I was haunted by what he had said. I would say that all of the military are proud to be doing a good job, but some obviously miss home and get desperately homesick.

While I was there, I was asked to go and visit the armoured tank regiment. These guys were at the cutting edge of the war, having a really tough time facing the threat of roadside bombs and the like. They are the soldiers who, every day, carry guns and wear loads of ammunition around their chests and body armour. When one of them put all his gear on to me, it was so heavy I nearly toppled over.

While I was with them, in an incredibly muddy field, I allowed as much time as I could for some photographic opportunities.

'Katherine, are you married?' one handsome, dark-haired soldier, who was about the same age as me, asked in the middle of all this.

'No, I'm single,' I replied, recalling that I had just recently split up with Steve.

'You're not married?'

'No.'

'You haven't even got a boyfriend?'

'No.'

'Right!'

At that, he turned to one of his friends and said: 'Hey, mate, give me your ring.' And, when this was handed over, he got down on one knee in the mud and said, 'Katherine, will you marry me?'

There must have been fifty men and women standing around, with him and me in the middle of this circle. His expression was totally serious, but I knew it was all being done in jest—at least I think it was—so I said, 'Okay, yes, I'll marry you,' and they all cheered. Throughout the rest of the day, whenever he saw me talking to someone else, he kept calling out, 'Hey, watch it—that's my missus.'

Gary Rhodes, the brilliant chef, was there to cook dinner for the troops, all 500 of them; as I really like to muck in when I go on these trips, I suggested to Joe Pasquale that we should act as the dinner-ladies. So, once Gary had cooked his delicious food, we stood behind the hot plates, dishing out the grub. All the guys were vying with each other, trying to get extra portions of roast potatoes and stuffing, but I wasn't showing any favouritism. That was all good fun, and Joe, who is a truly lovely man, was hysterical throughout.

When we'd first arrived in the morning, an officer had started to brief us on what to do if there was a mortar attack while we were at the base; but, as I was in charge of the group and could see from their faces that Gary, Joe and Kim from ITV were beginning to panic, I said to the officer: 'Hang on a minute, I thought mortar attacks only happened at night?'

'Yes,' he replied, 'that's true, usually after midnight or between two and three in the morning.'

'Then we needn't worry,' I said, 'because we're not going to be here then. We're leaving at midnight.'

Famous last words! Fate had other plans in store for us that night. After the last show, there we all were, packed up, ready to go, sitting in the little military airport waiting for our helicopter to take us back to Kuwait, when it began to dawn on us that we weren't going anywhere. A really dense fog had come in from nowhere and settled, and it was not long before we heard that one plane had already been grounded.

Within minutes, it was my turn to panic. I had a Montblanc photo shoot booked in for the day after we were due to get home, and I needed to get to Kuwait in order to get the flight back to the UK. I knew if the helicopter didn't come soon, we'd miss the flight, and I would be letting down a lot of people. Joe was also panicking. He had a dress rehearsal for his pantomime the next day, and if he didn't do the rehearsal he wouldn't be able to get any insurance cover.

There was nothing we could do, though, and within minutes, we got the news that we were dreading: we weren't going home and would have to spend the night in the barracks. At that moment, all my earlier reassuring words about mortar attacks began to evaporate and, without saying a word, Gary and Joe looked at each other, touching wood.

Having taken us to our rooms, the officer's parting words were, 'So if you hear the sirens go off, it means there's a mortar attack and you will need to get out of bed, put on your helmet and flak jacket and lie under the bed for at least forty minutes or until someone comes to get you.'

As I entered my room, bearing these instructions in mind, I was in for a shock. The first thing I saw was that my bed didn't have any legs and was, therefore, lying flatpack-style on the floor.

'Oh my gosh,' I muttered, 'what do I do if there is a mortar attack?'

But as there was nobody around to answer this

question, I just climbed into the bed wearing my flak jacket, placed my helmet on my chest, and tried to get some sleep. By army standards, the VIP room that I'd been given was a lovely ensuite room—and I hate complaining because I know how difficult things are in a war zone—but I was very tired and, apart from lying there worrying about mortar attacks, I was freezing cold. I put on every single item of clothing, including a coat that I had brought with me, but I was still covered in goosebumps and shivering all the time, and I hardly slept a wink. Fortunately, after a couple of fruitless hours tossing and turning, we were told that the fog was lifting and that we would be getting a helicopter out at eight o'clock.

At the appointed hour, we all reported to the Mess, but eight o'clock came and went and it was still too foggy; then, at nine, ten and eleven o'clock, it was a case of more of the same. So, we missed our flight to Kuwait and our flight home. Brian booked me another flight, a somewhat circuitous one, which meant that I had to fly from Kuwait to Beirut, from there to Paris, then on to London.

At last we were told the fog had lifted enough for a helicopter to come and get us, but then there was another hitch that kept us grounded at the base. Just as the helicopter was due to land, some fierce fighting broke out in another part of Iraq, so our helicopter was redirected to the conflict, and we had to wait another hour for another helicopter by which time I'd missed the second flight that Brian had arranged.

Having at last arrived in Kuwait and checked into a hotel for a couple of hours, I finally got a flight, the third one that had been booked, to take me from Kuwait to Dubai and then on to London. When I arrived at Dubai to change planes, only too aware that I'd arrived late, I went straight to check-in, but things were not to go smoothly there either.

Brian had booked a first-class ticket so that I could hopefully get some sleep between Dubai and London, but at check-in they told me that the flight was overbooked and, because I was late arriving, they had given my first-class seat to somebody else and I would now have to fly Economy.

'Can anything else go wrong?' I wondered, totally exhausted.

The extraordinary thing was that everything that could go wrong had gone wrong on that trip. For example, when we first arrived in Kuwait, all Gary Rhodes's cooking utensils, including ingredients like vanilla pods that he needed to cook with, had been confiscated by the airport officials. After that, when anything went wrong, Joe and I pulled a face and arched our eyebrows, which meant: 'Can anything else go wrong?' So, when I was told that my first-class seat had been given away and I was now in Economy, I couldn't resist texting Joe.

'Joe, my flight's been overbooked! I'm doing the face at you! x'

I eventually landed at London Heathrow at seven in the morning and was taken straight by car to Bryan Adams's house where we were due to start shooting the next campaign for Montblanc at nine o'clock.

By then I'd been up, without sleep, for two days—and I was supposed to be looking my best for the photo shoot. What I usually do before shoots is have a facial, get my nails done and have a good night's sleep, so that I can turn up looking my best. But, on this occasion, I hadn't had time for anything. I think I even turned up for the shoot still in my combats and muddy boots!

These photo shoots, which always involve a top-class photographer, lighting guys and assistants, make-up, hair and dress- stylists, cost the earth because there are so many people involved, and I felt I was letting everybody down. In some ways I was pleased to have made it there, but I honestly don't know how I got through that session. Now, when I look at Bryan's glamorous photos that have been circulated all over the world, I can appreciate what a good make-up artist, stylist, hairdresser and great photographer can do.

To this day, I am haunted by the petrified young man I met in Iraq. Long after I returned home, I kept hearing his voice, and, for at least two weeks, I dreamed of him every night and had nightmares about the situation he had found himself in. I know that sounds a somewhat dramatic reaction, but that's how it was. That young lad's face still remains the strongest image of my trips to Iraq.

*   *   *

Over the past four years when so many extraordinary things had happened to me, my mum had remained very laid-back. Proud, yes, she's a good Welsh mum, but she never went doolally about it—or at least not in front of me. I might have been singing in the famous Sydney Opera House, but she'd stay cool and say, 'Yes, you were great tonight.' Sometimes, but always for a joke, she'd say, 'Oh, you're *mega*, Katherine' or 'Oh, you're *cosmic*.' She was excited, really excited, by

230

all my successes, but she never went over the top about it, never jumped up and down, and I think that's what kept me so down-to-earth. However, when I did *Parkinson*, all that changed. I managed to get ten tickets for the show. I gave them to my mum, Laura and her boyfriend Gavin; my mum's sisters, my aunties Jo and Louise, and two of their daughters and some of my friends, Sophie, Ali and Katie.

On 23 December 2006, I appeared as a guest and performer and, apart from my spontaneous rendering of 'Going down the garden to eat worms', I sang the Welsh national anthem and a Christmas song, 'Have Yourself a Merry, Little Christmas', backed by the Fron Male Voice Choir and a brass band. I must say I was thrilled just to have got on to Parky's set; but it's the high heels, the long dress and those famous steps down to the studio floor that nearly do it for you on *Parkinson*. To make matters worse, I was wearing a dress that was very long, and, as I had to hitch this up with my hands, I couldn't hold on to the rail very well as I was walking down the steps. My first thought was 'Oh, please don't fall, Katherine. Not tonight!'

I took the steps very slowly, with as much dignity as I could muster while feeling terrified. After all, somebody had told me that Parky himself had tumbled down the stairs when a famous dancer was on the show. My second thought when I touched down safely was 'Oh, my God, I'm on Parky!' followed by *'Oh, my God! Oh, my God! Oh, my God!'*

At the end of my chat with Parky, during the commercial break, I remember looking out and seeing my mum's face. She was just staring at me,

231

mouth open, an expression of sheer astonishment on her face. Then, afterwards at the drinks reception, to which I took all the family because they all wanted to be introduced to Parky, Mum turned to me and, obviously freaking out, said: 'I can't believe it, Katherine, I can't believe it. How did this happen? You're my daughter and now you're like an international superstar!'

It was the first time she had fully acknowledged what had happened, and we both freaked out. Up until then, Mum had always said she didn't know how I coped and how I had adjusted so well, but I'm not sure I did adjust. I just went with the flow, got on with it. There were always so many great things coming up that I was always looking ahead and never had time to dwell on what was happening or had happened. It was a case of, 'Oh, now I've got to work for this,' or 'Learn the next lot of music and focus on that.' So I never really stopped or looked back or thought, 'Oh my gosh, that album went to number one' or 'Do you realise you were just singing with Tom Jones?'

I think if I had actually stopped and really looked at what was happening, like I am doing at this moment for my autobiography, I would have freaked out much sooner than I did that night of the *Parkinson* show.

I sing because I love it, but the very best bit is seeing how much my family enjoy everything that's happening. It is they who keep me grounded; and Neath is still my favourite place—and I'm as determined as ever not to change. I've often been asked if I have any really deep, personal concerns about the fact that the lives of so many successful people, such as singers and movie stars, seem to end in grief.

'No,' I reply. 'I must say it has never crossed my mind to worry about that.'

I guess I'm lucky because I've always known that I have a very strong family who are always there for me. I've always had the love and stability and that has given me the strength to do what I do: travel the world, be away from all those who are my nearest and dearest, and survive.

Sometimes, these days, when I go out with Laura to ordinary places we enjoy, people say 'What on earth are you doing here, Katherine?' and I think, 'Why not?' I don't want to lose my normal life. I still want to be able to do all those things. But, then, there are other times when I realise, 'Okay, maybe that's not possible any more.' After Christmas 2006, all this began to hit home—and it was being on *Parkinson* that made the difference.

NINETEEN

THE GOOSE IS COMING

My next BFF trip, this time to entertain the troops in Afghanistan, was planned for 23 December 2006, coming back on Christmas Eve. I've always believed that everything happens for a reason and I thought the recent complications of the trip to Iraq had happened to show me that the best-laid plans can go adrift. Nobody, for example, can determine the weather—fog can creep in like an uninvited guest—and there was a lesson for me to learn in all this.

For example, Christmas 2006 was an especially sensitive festive season for my family. It was Mum's first Christmas without Nanna and I had been told that Afghanistan was a notoriously difficult place to get both in and out of. 'If I get held up there,' I thought, 'it'll make things so much worse for Mum and Laura, and I really do feel they need me more than ever this year.' So, torn, though I was between visiting the troops and being with my family, I decided to delay going to Afghanistan until February 2007. I was very glad I made that decision: Mum, Laura and I really needed to be together that Christmas and New Year.

*   *   *

In February, a couple of days before we were due to take off for Afghanistan, Jim Davidson called.

'Hi there, GI Jenkins,' he said, 'are you ready for

off?'

'Yes, I am,' I stammered, 'but I must confess I'm a bit worried, Jim.'

'Don't worry,' he replied, 'the Goose is coming.'

'The Goose?' I queried. 'Who on earth is the Goose?'

'The Goose,' Jim said, in hyping-it-up mode, 'is just the greatest. This chap is legendary, has entered British military folklore. An ex-paratrooper, known as the hardest SAS man ever, he now looks after prominent people going into dangerous situations—and he's coming just to look after you.'

'Okay—cool,' I said, both reassured and flattered. And those words, 'the Goose is coming' stuck in my mind.

When I met 'the Goose' at Brize Norton, I saw what Jim had meant. He looked a hard case, was obviously not someone to mess with; was incredibly tall and muscular, built like a steel girder, but, despite his looks, he was a pussycat really—a real softie. Later, I learned that he had acquired the name 'Goose' when he was a biker and attached to a gang called 'The Outlaws'. I also learned that he was in the parachute regiment before going on to the SAS, and that while he was in the SAS he was awarded the military cross for being the personal bodyguard to General Rose in Bosnia.

Something else I soon learned on that trip was that the Goose hardly ever said a word; but I just knew instinctively that should anything untoward happen, he would be there; the one who would say: 'Right, Katherine. You just need to . . .' I guess the best bodyguards and security people are always those you hardly realise are there, and that's how the Goose was. He kept a watchful eye on me all the time, but stayed out of the way. Every now and again, though, I would venture, 'Hi, Goose.' I never did learn his real name.

One thing's for sure, though, you form an instant bond with anyone with whom you visit a war zone, which is why Jim Davidson and I are now such good friends. He is a shocker, though. He comes out with words and sayings I have never heard before in my life and they remain like scars on my mind. Then, just when I think I've managed to forget or erase them, I go away with him again.

When I arrived at Brize Norton, the largest station in the Royal Air Force, which employs nearly four thousand service personnel and over six hundred civilians, and deploys UK troops worldwide, I checked in, then went off to find a toilet. While I was drying my hands in there, a young lady dressed in full combats came out of the loos.

'Oh hello, Katherine,' she said, greeting me with a lovely smile, 'where are you off to?'

'Afghanistan,' I replied.

'Oh, I've just come back from there,' she said.

'How was it?' I asked.

'Horrendous. I came back on the plane with the wounded who weren't in a good state, moaning and groaning, God bless them.'

I was really pleased that conversation had taken place right at the beginning of the trip and, as soon as I left the toilets, I phoned Mum.

'Don't ever let me moan like that again. Honestly, I don't know I'm born sometimes.'

The plane that took us out was a Lockheed L-10 TriStar, which has very small, upright seats of the

236

most uncomfortable design imaginable, no in-flight entertainment system and just one dry sandwich on offer in nearly seven hours. Inside was a whole sea of desert-combat troops who were just going back into 'theatre', as they call it, after their leave, so the atmosphere was quite subdued.

The flight from Brize Norton to Qatar took six-and-a-half-hours, and we couldn't wait to get off the plane and stretch our legs. But that was not to be. When we landed, we were asked to remain seated on the plane, and we did that for at least an hour before a message finally came to us across the tannoy.

'We're terribly sorry everyone,' a disembodied voice announced, 'but as we landed the wheels of the plane caught fire, and I'm afraid we will have to continue to sit where we are until they cool down sufficiently for us to open the doors.' Not surprisingly, thoughts like: 'Oh, God, will the heat from the tyres cause the fuel tank to catch fire?' cascaded through my mind. But I tried to keep calm by reminding myself, as we continued to sit there, that we were in safe hands: the military were used to such emergencies, and, anyway, there were all those soldiers and the Goose on board to take care of us. Nevertheless . . .

For Tara Joseph, my newly appointed personal manager, who had only joined me a week before, this, her very first trip away with me, was truly— excuse the pun—a baptism of fire. Apart from being grilled alive, though, what I was most worried about was that the original schedule had only included a few hours sleep on arrival in what I knew would be a tiny army bunk bed on the base at Qatar before we had to get another flight from

Qatar to Kandahar, and even that short rest period had now been jeopardised. The flight to Kandahar, we'd been told, would take four and a half hours, then we'd change planes and fly on to Lashkar Gah where we were going to do the first show.

When at last the tyres were considered sufficiently cool to let us off the plane, I couldn't help thinking, as I glanced at Goose, whose face was as inscrutable as ever: 'For a moment back there, Goose, I thought my goose was cooked!'

Anyway, as a result of the wheels catching fire, I only got an hour and a half's sleep before getting on a Merlin from Qatar to Kandahar. The Merlins are huge, very powerful, noisy planes that have seats that run along both sides of the craft, so that the middle is a completely open space into which Land Rovers and tanks can be carried.

Once on board the Merlin, we had another two-hour journey on that and then a helicopter ride to the military base at Lashkar Gah. It was one of those occasions when I thanked God that I'd been on a helicopter before. At least this meant I knew roughly what to expect. They are rather scary things to be convoyed around in, but you do get used to them, which is just as well as they are the only way to travel in places like Afghanistan where road travel is far too dangerous.

We arrived at Lashkar Gah late, of course, with just forty-five minutes to spare before I was due to go on stage. At that point, I had no make-up on, hadn't done my hair—in fact, had really bad 'helmet hair'—hadn't got into my dress, hadn't done any scales to warm up my already dehydrated vocal cords, so it was just one mad dash to get ready. Yet, somehow, when I went on stage, I

238

managed to give one of the best shows I've ever done. My voice seemed to come from out of nowhere—and even I was stunned.

Immediately after the performance we were due to have lunch and, as it was such a lovely day, I decided to go outside, mingle with the soldiers, and sit in the sun with Tara, who was coping so well with having been thrown in the deep end. Picnic tables had been set up between the tents, our packed lunches were collected, and we sat down and had a really good laugh and some photos taken with a lovely group of marines. When I asked them how they were doing, several of them said: 'It's okay, but we lost one of our group last week.' I could tell the loss of that brave soldier was weighing very heavily on their minds.

'Certain parts of Afghanistan,' another told me, 'are very dangerous and the Taliban are really vicious in their attacks. It's the suicide bombers,' he added, 'and some of the injuries our lads have sustained have been horrific. There was also a mortar attack here on the base last night.'

Tara and I were allocated an area in the women's quarters to get ready that evening; it consisted of a large tent with pods going off long corridors, and each pod contained six camp-beds. I was astonished. The soldiers didn't have any space that they could call their own. Their camp-bed is their only personal space, and I was so impressed, despite the incredibly cramped conditions, by how well everyone seemed to get on.

By chance, one of the women was somebody I had met and admired on my first visit to Basra. A lovely intensive-care nurse, she was now in Afghanistan to go out on the helicopters to pick up the wounded after the Taliban attacks.

'The things I am seeing here,' she said, obviously distressed, 'are unbelievable, Katherine. Far worse than in Iraq.' She was my hero.

Having done the show in Lashkar Gah, we flew by helicopter over the Afghan desert to Camp Bastion, in Helmand province, where there were 4,000 men and 200 women serving. On that occasion, we learned we were flying in a convoy of two helicopters: ours in front and another behind us carrying Air Chief Marshal Sir Jock Stirrup, Head of the British Armed Forces, who was spending the day going around the different bases.

'You do realise,' Jim said cheerfully, 'that our helicopter is a decoy for the general's helicopter.'

'Charming!' I replied.

I always think the best way to get an idea of a country is to fly over it. Iraq, for example, is as flat as a pancake, but every now and again there are little settlements where people live and sometimes the children run out and wave up at you. In Afghanistan, though, the only thing to be seen are tiny buildings that have been reduced to rubble, and there are huge bomb craters everywhere. Occasionally you might glimpse a man walking across a vast area of mountainous sand dunes with a camel, and you can follow his footprints in the sand.

'Where on earth can he be walking to and from?' I asked myself.

I had the feeling that he had been walking for weeks; there was no other sign of life for as far as the eye could see.

For our show at Camp Bastion, the troops had built a raised stage. I think it was the best show that

Jim and I had ever done together. Jim, who was on top form that day, went on first and kept telling jokes about me that I can't repeat because, if I did, my mum would kill him, and me for repeating it. He is absolutely brilliant at winding up the troops and I have to say that, even though I have heard his act many times now, his timing was just perfect that night and he was particularly funny.

By the time I went on it was all wolf-whistles, drumming of feet and catcalls. I started chatting to them and, as they were heckling me, I heckled them back. After singing a couple of songs, I took a pause and told them that I had been on *Parkinson* just before I came out and had mentioned that I was coming to Afghanistan. 'After that,' I told them, 'people kept stopping me in the street and saying, "Please tell the boys and girls out there that we're really, really proud of them".

'I'm really proud of you, too,' I added. 'You're my inspiration and I want to dedicate the last song of the show to you. It's called, "(Everything I do), I do it for you".'

As I said that, they all jumped to their feet and applauded, and I was so overwhelmed I could hardly sing a note.

I should explain that the crowd in front of me was split into two, with an aisle down the middle, and I was on a raised stage; as I started singing the song, one of the marines walked up to the stage and stood in front of me, while a friend took his photograph with me in the background—and this really started something. A couple more followed, then, during the guitar solo in the song, another got up and spread his arms out, so that it seemed that I was singing in his arms. Then, just before I got to

241

the very last bit of the song, where it goes into 'You know it's true . . . everything I do . . .' another guy jumped up on to the edge of the stage, sat down and started singing with me, and everyone applauded him.

'I've got to work with this one,' I thought, so I knelt down beside him, put an arm around him and sang the line 'you know it's true . . . everything I do . . .' at which point he grabbed the mike off me and said, 'I would do it for you, Kath'. And the whole of Camp Bastion just erupted. It was great, and we sang the last phrase 'I do it for you' together. The troops went mental. It was the best rapport ever.

Having left the stage, I signed as many autographs as I could, but I was mobbed. There were so many of them and they all wanted their picture taken. It was such a lovely feeling, and I've now got great pictures of me surrounded by the troops. It was just *fab-lous*, a brilliant atmosphere.

Then we said our goodbyes, jumped on to the helicopter and eventually made the journey back to London, via Dubai, and landed on time.

*   *   *

Dame Vera's ninetieth birthday celebration, held at the Imperial War Museum in London on 20 March 2007, was a very special occasion. Baroness Thatcher was there along with Lord Slim, the president of the Burma Star Association, Lord Tebbit, Baroness Boothroyd, Lady Soames, the politician Ann Widdecombe, writer Jilly Cooper, actor Edward Fox, actress Dora Bryan, entertainers Liz Smith, June Whitfield, Darcey Bussell, Bill

Pertwee, Roy Hudd, and many other celebs from all walks of life. As part of the celebration, I was invited along to sing some of the songs that Dame Vera had made famous, such as 'We'll Meet Again' and 'White Cliffs of Dover' and then lead guests into a chorus of 'Happy Birthday'.

While Dame Vera and I were being interviewed for Sky News that day, we were asked, 'How different do you think your roles as Forces Sweethearts are—or are they the same?'

'Basically,' I replied, 'they are the same: to go out among the troops and tell them that everyone is very proud of them at home and let them know that they are not forgotten, and just do what we can to cheer them up and boost morale.'

Soon after I returned from that recent trip to Afghanistan, I was very touched to receive the following letter addressed to *Katherine Jenkins, Forces Special Sweetheart*, from Commando Logistic Regt Camp Bastion, BFPO 792, and dated 14 February 2007. Here is an extract from it:

Wow! What an amazing performance you gave to us all here at Camp Bastion, Afghanistan. It was certainly a night to remember and a welcome break from the daily stress of the operational environment.

We all appreciated the wholehearted energy and fun that you exhibited throughout the entire visit. It was an uplifting experience for us all and refreshing to see a superstar enjoying time spent meeting and greeting the boys. You have a huge aura and such a gifted talent . . . the vocal range you can produce is absolutely formidable!

I would like to thank you very much for the

emotional heart-felt performance. You really gauged the feelings of everyone out here, especially following Christmas and so close to Valentine's Day. You may not be aware but many of the audience comprised of different elements of the UK armed forces. Sat in front of me were six Royal Marines and an RAF Apache pilot who had just come in off special operations, still parading full-length beards, who had been encountering daily 'contacts' with enemy Taliban forces, living in trenches and eating boil-in-the-bag rations three times a day. The next minute they are sat in front of Katherine Jenkins! What a culture shock!!

Some of these guys had unfortunately lost mates in action, whilst others had been flown home severely ill. Coincidentally, sat behind me were some of the UK's leading Tri-Service Consultant Surgeons, Anaesthetists and Physicians who had spent the previous hectic two weeks undertaking life-saving operations. Many people also do not realise that not only are UK troops treated by medics in the field-hospital facility but also the Afghan National Army, Police, civilians, local contractors and enemy forces!

The British Forces Foundation is a great charity that Jim has founded and I hope that you will continue in your capacity as Trustee. Please keep up the great work that you are doing. It's an absolutely brilliant show that you both put together. With Jim's squaddie humour which goes down so well and your amazing performance, it really is an excellent night of top-class entertainment.

This letter is one that I will never forget and will always keep as a reminder of my BFF trips.

TWENTY

SO MUCH SO SOON . . .

Hercules, TriStars, Merlins, jeeps, tanks, Land Rovers, helmets, flak jackets in recent days; and now, back in London, a horse-drawn carriage, complete with the young handsome Peruvian tenor, Juan Diego Flórez. After my recent dramatic experiences in helicopters and planes in Iraq and Afghanistan, I couldn't wait to get back down to earth, if that's how the star-studded occasion that is the Classical BRITs can be described. As for Juan Diego Flórez, he certainly looked like a prince to accompany me on my fairytale journey from the Royal Garden Hotel, Kensington, to the Royal Albert Hall in Kensington Gore.

The line-up for the 2007 BRITs could not have been more exciting or, for that matter, more youthful. It was positively bursting at the seams with young talented people; and included among these was Juan Diego Flórez, who had recently made history by responding to the audience and giving the first encore at La Scala since 1933; Chinese pianist Lang Lang, the violinists Joshua Bell and Nicola Benedetti; and, unbelievably, for the third year running, I'd been nominated for the Album of the Year Award.

When it comes to the BRITs, all the record companies know the week before the actual red-carpet event who has actually won the various awards, but they rarely inform their stars. In previous years, Brian and Universal Classics, my

246

record label, knew I had won, but they chose to put me off the scent and tell me otherwise. They did this so that the television cameras could catch the best genuine natural reaction from me when the announcement was made on the night. So, in 2006, Brian told me that Amy Nuttall had won; and in 2005, he told me that Sir James Galway had won. And, on both those occasions, trusting person that I am, I was utterly convinced that I had not won the award for Album of the Year, and my reaction was certainly genuine when I heard that I had.

The year 2007, however, did not follow the usual format. In May, when Brian told me that Sir Paul McCartney would win the Album of the Year award—always the BRITs' most hotly contested category—I knew he was telling the truth this time.

All that aside, the 2007 BRITs were fantastic. I had been in serious training with Sean, my trainer, who very nearly killed me three times a week. But, as I wanted to look my absolute best, I grinned and bore it. No pain, no gain. Then it was a case of choosing what to wear, which I always find a challenge because I like to avoid the obvious.

In 2007, since I had arrived for the previous four years of the BRITs in very glamorous dresses, I chose a turquoise all-in-one jump suit, made by Maria Grachvogel. It was a really fun choice and I wore it with matching handbag and shoes by Jimmy Choo, topped it off with Montblanc's new Etoile collection of jewellery, and I wore a necklace with twenty-two carat diamonds in it and matching earrings. The necklace alone cost a breath taking £1.6 million. So, yes, I did feel a million-plus dollars wearing it.

Juan Diego Flórez and I decided we'd go do the

red carpet bit together, hence the sharing of the open-topped, horse-drawn carriage. I hadn't seen Juan Diego, who is a good friend of mine, since we had met up in New York several months before, so we had plenty to chat about as the horses clip-clopped their way to the Royal Albert Hall; and, for some of the way, we were actually writing the repertoire list for my Kathfest festival later in the year—at which, great thrill, Juan Diego (who I think is the world's best young tenor) had agreed to perform. Meanwhile the photographers were running along beside the carriage clicking away.

I had been given the great honour of opening the show (wearing an amazing red dress, made for me by the Kruszynska sisters) by singing 'World In Union', which was then followed by the Fron Male Voice Choir singing the Welsh national anthem. I was so moved when all the audience in the Royal Albert Hall stood up for this.

I was really pleased to be opening the show because that meant, having done my bit, I could sit down at our table with the people from Universal and enjoy the rest of the proceedings. First, though, after opening the show I had to go and meet the press. They all knew that Sir Paul had won the 'Album of the Year' award, and kept asking me how I felt about that, so I had to be especially diplomatic.

The Duchess of Cornwall is the patron of the Classical BRIT awards and I was told that she wanted to meet me during the interval. I'd sung for her before, but had never actually met her. When I did, I thought she was lovely, absolutely delightful. Also in the room at that time was the television presenter, Katie Derham, Aled Jones and Sting with his wife, Trudie Styler.

At one point, Camilla asked me if I spoke Welsh and when I said yes she added: 'Do many people in Wales speak it?'

'It depends where they live really,' I replied. 'Welsh is compulsory in schools now until the age of fourteen, so I speak it, but my mother doesn't.'

'My husband speaks a little Welsh,' she added, obviously proud of Prince Charles, 'and I'm always very impressed when he sings the Welsh national anthem in Welsh.' She paused, then added: 'I'd love to learn the words of that.'

'Well,' I said, 'if you ever need some lessons I will gladly teach you.'

'I might need some singing lessons before that,' she laughed.

'Funnily enough,' I replied, 'I could help you with that, too.'

I also met the brilliant young violinist Joshua Bell, who had performed a spellbinding rendition of 'Summer' from Vivaldi's *The Four Seasons*, and the incredibly energetic, full of life young pianist, Lang Lang. In fact, what I loved about the 2007 BRITs was that so many of the mega-talented artists were so young, which was great because we all went off to party afterwards.

*   *   *

Two days after the Classical BRITs, I went on my first ever visit to China, and I loved it. We arrived in Beijing in the morning and, as the only thing I had to do that day was to go for a sound-check for Montblanc's gala dinner, Tara and I had a tour guide to show us around.

249

The first place we went to was Tiananmen Square. I couldn't help but think of the student demonstration and the iconic photograph of a lone man standing in front of a tank.

From there, we went to the Forbidden City, which was just across the road. I couldn't believe how massive it was and the huge walls that surround it made me feel very small and insignificant. In contrast to the awful events in the Square, the names of the emperors' palaces suggested harmony and peace. For example: Palace of Highest Harmony, Gate of Heavenly Purity, Palace of Longevity—and many more.

'It's called the Forbidden City,' the guide told us, 'because it was home to the Chinese emperors for about 500 years, and only their servants and Chinese royalty were allowed in during that time. For anyone else who tried to enter, the penalty was death.'

The following day I went to do the TV show *Wanna Challenge?* which has 400 million viewers. This show was filmed in a brand new theme park called Happy Valley, in Beijing. The idea of the theme park is to show off many different parts of the world—and I was in the Greek section, singing in a ruined coliseum.

There were only about two thousand people in the audience, and the organisers insisted I enter in an open-topped stretched Audi, with the bodyguards walking alongside it, as I waved to the huge crowd. It was all somewhat bizarre, and I felt a bit like the Queen!

It's very important for me, whenever I go to another country, to try to learn a little bit of the language. So, as I was about to speak Chinese for the very first time in front of 400 million viewers, I decided, just before I opened my mouth to sing, to say 'Hello' to the host, 'hello to everybody at home', and 'I love you all' to the audience—all in Chinese. The audience went nuts and I really enjoyed that.

It was such a shame that we had to get the flight home at five o'clock the next morning, because the programme was not going out until about eleven o'clock that night.

'If only you were staying here just one more day,' the organiser of the show said, 'you would not be able to walk down the street after doing this show.'

I really loved my visit there. The people were very friendly, and I'd like to go back there for a concert tour in the near future.

The month of May was not finished for me yet. There was still another surprise in store for my family and fans, which had come about as a result of a charity performance I had done at a benefit for the Anthony Nolan Bone Marrow Trust, where I met all the cast of *Emmerdale*.

Having spent some time chatting to members of the cast, I thought they were all lovely, and I stayed in touch with the programme's producer and directors. Then, in 2007, I was asked if I would like to have a cameo role in *Emmerdale*.

'That sounds fun,' I thought. 'Nobody would expect me to pop up in that series.' Plus it was my Nanna's all-time favourite TV show and I couldn't help thinking that it would have made her so proud. All I had to do, apparently, was play myself in two episodes, which were being transmitted for half an hour on 16 May 2007 and an hour the following day.

The storyline was for me to appear as myself to open *Emmerdale*'s five-hundredth anniversary pageant, and the script included a big build-up and dialogue about whether the villagers would really be able to get me, a celebrity, to come and open the pageant. They couldn't quite believe I would come, but I did and, amid all the other *Emmerdale* shenanigans, including the death of one of its best-loved characters, I met everybody, declared the pageant open, then sang 'Time to Say Goodbye' over the credits at the close of the show.

It really was a laugh, but it was weird watching myself on TV like that, and it certainly didn't make me want to change my career plans. I would still much rather be a singer than an actress any day.

*   *   *

One occasion I'd been holding my breath for was a very prestigious event I'd been invited to attend in St Petersburg, in, of all places, Catherine the Great's palace. This occasion was attended by all the rich-list people in Russia, but what made it truly special for me was that the orchestra I was performing with was conducted by Maestro Valery Gergiev who, in my view and the view of many others, is one of the best conductors in the world. I couldn't have been more thrilled when I heard that I would be working with him.

Having said that, I was also very apprehensive. Conductors just don't get better than Maestro Valery Gergiev and, of all the luck, this was destined to be the first big prestigious concert I had ever done in a large venue without the use of amplification. I needn't have worried, though; the

252

Maestro couldn't have been more reassuring and encouraging and, in the event, despite all my fears, my voice reached all those at the back.

As part of the White Nights Festival, Montblanc was sponsoring a new annual award, called 'The New Voices Award' to honour and recognise new talent. They gave Maestro Valery Gergiev the task of deciding whom he thought was worthy of receiving it and also asked him to present it to the person he had chosen.

To my great surprise and delight, the Maestro decided I should receive the award during its inaugural year. I couldn't have felt more honoured to be chosen to receive the award by such a man.

Included in the songs I sang at my recital were the 'Habanera' and 'Chanson Bohème' from *Carmen*, and 'Mon coeur s'ouvre a ta voix' from *Samson and Delilah*. The following evening we had the ball at Katherine the Great's Palace and all the staff were dressed as if they had just stepped off the set of *Amadeus*, and a fanfare called us all into dinner. I really felt as if I was living in another era.

The vast Great Hall, sometimes also called the Light Gallery, where receptions, celebrations, dinners, balls and masquerades are held, is full of Russian baroque-style gilded mirrors, and has a breathtakingly beautiful ceiling on which figures, contained within painted colonnades, float around on a backdrop of blue sky. It was yet another event that I will remember all my life.

I can hardly begin to describe what a special occasion those two days and nights proved to be; I've never experienced anything quite like them. I will never forget going out on to the terrace of the palace and seeing all the walkways of the tiered gardens lit up by flaming torches, then watching one of the most magnificent firework displays I have ever seen.

Another wonderful part of that trip was when we were invited up to a beautiful balcony-cum-veranda for drinks and I sat there surrounded by young Russian billionaires, listening to a couple of them arguing about who was going to give me a lift home in their private jet. It really was insane, hysterical, hilarious. I loved it all so much—the lavish dinner, the concert and the magnificent ball—that I told Brian I want to go again next year.

I could have been forgiven for thinking that trip to St Petersburg was excitement enough for one year, but there was more to come, and I can still hardly believe that, while I was writing this book, Placido Domingo, one of my all-time heroes, invited me to be his special guest at the Panathenaic Stadium in Athens, where the first-ever modern-day Olympic Games were held.

I just couldn't wait to get to Athens to sing duets with him; and my heart skipped a beat when, just before I was due to do this, he called me at home one night and said in his slow Spanish purr: 'Hello Ka-the-rine, this is Pla-ci-do, I want to talk to you about our repertoire.'

The concert, which took place just a couple of days after I returned from Russia, was, in my view, one of the best concerts I've ever done, even though it took place in the middle of an incredible heatwave. My mother, I'm beginning to think, is a bad omen. I love taking her with me to places she wants to go, but whenever I do, something out of the ordinary always seems to happen. In Miami, for example, there was a hurricane and we had to evacuate; then, when I take her with me to Greece, because she really wants to see Athens, a heatwave of forty-seven degrees kicks in and it was so hot we couldn't even leave the hotel. The concert was due to start at 9 p.m., but we didn't go on stage until at least 10.30 because it was too hot for the instruments to be played.

For our duets, Placido and I sang *The Merry Widow Waltz*, *Non ti scordar di me*, 'If I Loved You' from *Carousel* and 'Tonight' from *West Side Story*. 'Tonight' was my favourite to sing because it's such a passionate duet and Placido's voice is just incredible. As we sang it, he had his arms around me and the fact that I could feel his breathing as his voice soared was the highlight of the evening. I just loved working with him, and we finished the concert with *Saro per te*, a duet that was written especially for us by Placido's son, Placido Junior.

I can't say often enough what a gentleman Placido is: every time I went on stage, he took me by the hand and led me on, but one particular moment that sums up for me his phenomenal charm occurred at the end of the evening. As we came out of the stadium after the concert, both our cars moved forward at the same time, but, just as Placido's car was about to go through the gates, he realised my car was behind his. The next moment the reverse lights of his car came on and, as the car reversed all the way back until it was alongside my car, he wound down the window and said: 'Ladies first.' I loved that moment!

Placido is also a very generous man. He gave all the proceeds of the Athens concert to help the millions of refugee children of Darfur.

When I came off stage that night in Athens, I'd

had such a fantastic show, and enjoyed myself so much, that, despite the heat, some energy flooded back into my body and I couldn't resist running the track. So, having changed into shorts and trainers, which were, fortunately, in one of the bags I had with me, I said to Brian, who used to run marathons, 'Come on, Brian, you can't be in an Olympic Stadium and *not* run the track'—and, ever willing to rise to a challenge, he ran the 400-metre track with me, still dressed in his suit. It was hysterical!

As we were jogging along some members of the audience, who were coming down from the stands, started to walk across the track and they were astonished when they saw it was me running. All of a sudden, one guy, who started sprinting alongside me, called out, 'Miss Jenkins, can I have your autograph?'

'Yes,' I replied, feeling just like my hero, Forrest Gump, 'but not until I get to the end of the track.'

Then, just as we came round the last bend, all these paparazzi appeared from nowhere. Even then, although I now had eight men running in front of me, I was absolutely determined to keep on running: 'Nobody's going to stop me, I'm going to finish this.'

Then, to my utter astonishment, I saw Placido running towards me and, as I ran towards him and gave him a big hug, he said: 'Finish, Katherine, finish'; and, as I continued, one of his grandsons, who was taking photographs, captured an amazing photograph of me running the Olympic track with Placido running after me. No moment could beat that!

The following day I had calls from my family,

saying: 'Oh, my God, you're on the front page of all the Welsh papers in your running shorts', and I was mortified because, like most women I don't think my legs are all that great and I hate seeing photographs of myself in shorts.

It just goes to show, though, what a high I must have been on that night to be able to run that 400-metre track after doing a show-of-a-lifetime in the middle of a heatwave.

One way or another, one high was destined to follow another during the year I was writing this book; and the next one, a very important event that I'd been dreaming about for a very long time, was my one-day 2007 music festival, 'Katherine in the Park'—nicknamed 'Kathfest' by the press.

This was held at Margam Park, near Port Talbot, which was the nearest possible venue to our home in Neath, and a place to which Mum and Dad used to take Laura and me for weekends in the caravan when we were children.

Margam Park, complete with an abbey and deer running around, is a very beautiful setting, really *gor-geous*, and, as it is situated just off the M4, it was a very convenient venue for my music festival. Having said that, I had already received letters from people all over the world, telling me they would be coming.

It had been one of the wettest summers on record and for a week before the great day I was really stressed about the weather and kept praying. Like Glastonbury, my festival was an open-air event, so the entire audience was obviously going to be exposed to the elements.

'If it's horrible, especially if there's torrential rain and thunder and lightning, nobody will come,'

I wailed inwardly, 'and my first festival will be a wash-out.'

Miraculously, though, on the afternoon of the performance, the sun came out and I couldn't have asked for a better day. The sky was blue, with perfect pink-and-white fluffy clouds scudding around. It all looked unbelievably beautiful.

My dream from the start had been to create a festival that united world-class artists from all different genres to come to my area of south Wales to perform; and I hoped that the festival would be so successful that it would become an annual event thereafter. And I succeeded.

Among the performers was my dear friend, Juan Diego Flórez, plus the National Symphony Orchestra, conducted by Anthony Inglis, Serendipity, and Paul Potts, the recent winner of the TV show *Britain's Got Talent*, who comes from the part of Wales where Margam Park is situated.

I'd been playing with the idea of setting up my own festival for at least three years, and the fact that it actually happened, and the sun shone in a year when we never saw so much rain, was yet another dream come true. So many people in Wales had encouraged me in my singing and given me the opportunity to prove myself that I was left with a passionate need to give something back to them, especially the people of south Wales, who mean the world to me. When you have been given so much, and have had the kind of success I have had, I honestly think it's your duty to give something special back. The festival was my way of doing this.

On the day, I was so inspired by the audience, who were so lovely, warm and encouraging, that the following week I started making plans for next year's 'Kathfest', which will be a weekend festival. Thereafter I want to build it up to a three-day event. I want all the festivals to be a fun weekend out for everybody and to appeal to all age groups with tastes ranging across the entire musical spectrum, from pop and rock to jazz to soul to country to classical.

Meanwhile I was thrilled with the press cuttings, like the one from the *South Wales Evening Post* that had the headline 'Stars Hit a High Note in the Park' and went on to read:

The weather that has hit so many events this summer stayed fine. People had been told to come prepared for rain. A dark threatening cloud hovered above the stage, but when the radiant Katherine, who comes from just down the road at Neath, appeared on stage, robed in a brilliant white gown, the weather brightened up right on cue. 'It's not raining,' Katherine beamed, then loud applause broke out as she revealed she was wearing pink Wellingtons beneath the gown. She then got the crowd on her side by saying: 'There are two kinds of people in this world. People who are Welsh and people who wish they were Welsh!'

I honestly don't think I could have enjoyed myself any more than I did. There wasn't one damp squib all day or evening and the fireworks at the end of the concert were absolutely spectacular—a perfect end to my first 'Kathfest'.

EPILOGUE

'WHAT NOW, LOVE?'

One object that travels around with me everywhere is a key-ring that has the Jenkins' family motto, *'Go forward but cautiously'* inscribed on it—and I guess that just about sums me up. I always want to move forward, but I'm not impulsive. For me, everything has to be carefully thought out.

So, what about my future? Have I, as some of the media will doubtless soon suggest, done it all, had it all? Am I, aged twenty-seven, ready to retire? Not me. I'm absolutely bursting with ideas and plans.

For a start I couldn't be more excited about my current project *Viva La Diva*, a show I am doing in tandem with the prima ballerina, and long-time heroine of mine, Darcey Bussell, whom I first met at the South Bank Awards a couple of years back. I love ballet, have always gone as often as I can, and have always thought Darcey, whom I have seen perform many times, to be an absolutely breathtaking ballerina. When I came on to the scene, I was thrilled when we kept bumping into each other at the same events.

During one of our lovely chats, we discovered that both of us, and our business managers, were thinking of putting on a show that would combine dance and music. Then, one day at lunch, Darcey and I came up with the idea for a joint show that would illustrate how every artist in the history of the arts has been inspired by another artist or artists; and that this inspiration is often the defining moment for what they want to achieve.

Convinced that this applied to every artist—that if, for example, we were to ask Robbie Williams or Placido Domingo, they would be sure to come up with the name of somebody who had inspired them—Darcey and I started playing around with this idea, and talking about who and what had been our inspirations. I was really surprised to hear some of hers, which were Audrey Hepburn, Ginger Rogers and Fred Astaire, Cyd Charisse, and she was likewise surprised by my inspirations: Marilyn Monroe, Doris Day, Judy Garland, Natalie Wood, Shirley Bassey and Barbra Streisand.

This, then, became the basis for our show: if we were surprised by our choices of who and what had inspired us, others would be, too, and that could make for a really interesting show, a show that would give us the chance to re-live our fantasies on stage. And that was how *Viva La Diva* came into being.

Everybody will doubtless guess that I will be doing the Marilyn Monroe number, 'Diamonds Are A Girl's Best Friend', but they might not guess that Darcey is going to be dancing in the style of Ginger Rogers, something nobody has ever seen her do before.

I also have a few surprises up my sleeve, which include some dancing. In fact, both of us will be stepping out of our comfort zones; and, right now, I'm having intensive dance classes because both Darcey and I will be ending the show with a big Busby-Berkeley-style tap routine.

I've enjoyed dancing all my life and, at various times, have done tap, jazz, modern and even a bit of ballet. All this activity really helped my posture, which needed some help because I was born with a slight curvature in my spine and a 'twisted ribcage', which regularly gives me a bad back and creates difficulties for me when I wear corseted dresses.

Broadway and Las Vegas, I am delighted to say, have already expressed an interest in *Viva La Diva*, and Darcey and I are planning to take this show worldwide. I'm so pleased we are doing this together because, when Darcey retired in June 2007 from the Royal Ballet Company, the company she had been dancing with for twenty glittering years, she was quoted as saying, 'Having devoted six days a week to ballet for so many years, to suddenly stop dancing altogether would be too much of a shock for me to bear.'

As for me, I know why I am so delighted to be doing the show, and that's because I am never happier than when I'm faced with something new and I find myself with a fresh challenge to work for. And boy, is this one going to be a challenge!

So, almost as soon as I finish writing this book, I will be doing all that, plus recording my new album, which is called *Rejoice*. Although I will be keeping to my classical roots for this, my fifth album—and there will, of course, be the hymns and arias that people have come to expect from me—it is also going to be even more crossover than my previous albums, and will include some brand new songs that have been especially written for me by Gary Barlow and Steve Mac. The cover photograph for this album has already been taken by Rankin, the great portrait and fashion photographer.

I've always said that I'll never make a move into pop, but I do love songs like 'Time To Say

Goodbye' that I have recorded in the past because, although it is a pop song, it has a classical feel and I'm always looking for other songs like that—songs in popular style that I can sing in my classical voice.

Having received so many letters from people telling me that my music has brought comfort to them during difficult times, I felt I wanted to record more inspirational songs, songs with a real message of hope and strength that would lift people's hearts. And I must say I've found great comfort myself in some of the new inspirational songs that I've recorded, in particular the words of 'Rejoice'. Although this year has been an absolutely wonderful year for me on the career front, it has also been a very hard one in my personal life. After nearly six years with Steve, I've spent 2007 getting used to being on my own again; but, today, fourteen months on, I finally feel back to my old self and for that, I rejoice. What was lost is found.

I am still living the dream, still thrilled and loving every minute of it, but there have also been times when I've pushed myself beyond the limit and ended up feeling completely drained and exhausted. My note to myself this year is that I have to learn to say no sometimes. I get so many invitations and, as much as I would like to do everything, there just aren't enough hours in the day. I really don't want to burn out. But, and there is always another but, isn't there, having said that, there are still lots of people on my wish list that I would love to work with in the future: Andrea Bocelli, Sir Tom Jones, Kanye West, Madonna, Sir Elton John and Take That for a start.

In the meantime, I shall be keeping one eye on

my cherished ambition for the future, which is to sing the title role in the opera *Carmen*. My heart has been totally set on playing that role for such a long time now: before I got my record deal, I did an amateur version in Wales and I really enjoyed it. I know it inside out and I just can't wait to do it professionally. To this end, I am still working with Beatrice Unsworth, my singing teacher from the Royal Academy, and I'm hoping if I keep training my voice, then I'll be ready for a full operatic role by the time I am thirty—three years from now.

I realise that when I do this, I may well be up against a problem or two. Because of the direction my career has taken thus far, the opera world might treat me with some scepticism and close ranks. This is why, when I decide the moment is right for me to start performing operatic roles, I want to be sure my voice is truly ready and that I haven't left any room for criticism. There are some who say, 'Once you have crossed over, that's it. You will never be allowed to cross back.' But I'm a determined young lady and I know, by now, that if my heart is really set upon something, I'm a force to be reckoned with.

As well as my favourite opera, *Carmen*, I am also a big fan of Mozart operas, such as *Cosi Fan Tutte* and *The Marriage of Figaro*, and the great romantic operas, such as Verdi's *La Traviata* and Puccini's *Tosca* and *La Bohème*. I like to go to Covent Garden and other opera houses whenever I can to listen to performances of these.

Meanwhile, I still offer no apology for having taken a more commercial route thus far. As far as I am concerned, crossover is a very useful stepping stone for getting people into classical music, something that was confirmed for me when I was in Wales one Christmas talking to some rugby players.

'All right, Kath?' one asked me. 'Saw you on the Classic FMTV the other day.'

'Don't tell me you watch that!' I laughed. 'You're pulling my leg, aren't you?'

'No, we do watch it,' he and some of the others replied. 'We like it because they also play soundtrack music from films like *Gladiator* and *Braveheart*.'

And the more we chatted the more I became aware that when people tune into something like Classic FMTV, and are introduced to the kind of classical crossover songs that I do, they are also introduced to classics like Vivaldi's *Gloria* and *The Four Seasons*. How great is that! It just goes to show that crossover serves a purpose, is a gateway. If somebody buys my album and is turned on to buying a CD of *Carmen*, or inspired to go to Covent Garden to see it, then surely this will help to keep classical music alive and encourage more young people to listen to it.

I honestly think it is very short-sighted to be precious or exclusive and snobbish about these things. I came from a very ordinary working-class background in Wales and, from time to time, I remember coming up against the idea that 'opera is only for the posh or well-off', which did sometimes make me feel uncomfortable. I don't want anybody else to feel like that.

So, okay, when I do opera for the first time I know I will be on trial, on probation so to speak, but that's all the more reason for me to go for it and do it to the best of my ability.

Another ambition of mine that has been around

for some time now is that I would love to test my skills on the *Top Gear* test track. I enjoy driving so much, am quite an assertive driver and, as I've lived in London for eight years now, where you need to be confident, I reckon I could give the other celebrity drivers a run for their money.

I really do want to get married one day—and married in my home church—because that kind of full-on commitment is very important to me. My mum and dad were together for twenty-five years, married for fifteen, and were very much in love and happy. So I have them as my role models and I know that with the right person, love can endure. I really do believe in loyalty, commitment and fidelity, and I want to go through life with one person who knows me better than anyone else. I want to make the silver and golden weddings, and, if I met the right person today, I would go for it. I also want to have kids—at least two or three.

At the moment I don't have time to get lonely, but I do miss having somebody special in my life. Since my last relationship, though, things have become even more complicated. In those days, there wasn't so much to take into account. Nowadays, and it's a horrible thing to say, I question *why* somebody would want to be involved with me, and feel I have to be careful. Is it really *me* they are interested in, or the image? Those doubts have definitely made the possibility of dating somebody more complex.

Every week, of course, the tabloid journalists call up and say: 'This is who *we* think is your new boyfriend . . .' (I think I've been linked to the entire Welsh rugby team by now) and, more often than not, I've never even met the person they're rattling on about. Sometimes they even team me up with Fadi, my hairdresser, who clearly has no interest in me, or any other woman for that matter. I don't think they can accept that I can go this length of time without having a boyfriend, but the truth is I haven't dated anybody seriously since Steve and I broke up in 2006.

I will gladly answer any questions that I am asked but I'm also determined to keep my personal life private. I've never been one for flaunting my private life, and even when Steve and I were living together we never really attended things together in public and certainly never spoke to the press about what we did 'at home'. I would never, for example, sell my wedding day to a glossy magazine. So, sorry guys, put away your pens and recorders, there will be no kiss 'n' tells from me.

The older I get, the better I understand my own character, my strengths and weaknesses, which is just as well because journalists keep asking me to describe myself for their columns.

What I usually say is, 'I think I am, first and foremost, a very affectionate person who always tries to take into consideration how other people might be feeling in any given situation. I try to do as many fun things as I can, because I love a good giggle and think laughter is the best cure for anything. Sometimes, however, I take myself, and life, a little too seriously, and let the stress get on top of me. Then I have to take a step back and say "Hey, Katherine, chill out. Enjoy!"'

In general, though, I'm a really happy person who loves life and, far from living in isolation, I live in north London, in an arca that is like a small village, where I know my neighbours and local shopkeepers. Having come from Neath, a sense of community is hugely important to me.

If you are in my life and one of my friends, then I will give you everything I have. In return I need truth, loyalty and honesty from the people who are close to me. When people are not honest with me, I find that really hard to deal with. If somebody has made a mistake, though, and puts up their hands and admits this, I am, I hope, forgiving—because, let's face it, we all make mistakes. If, however, somebody lies to me on a regular basis, I will walk away.

I am not really impressed by how well somebody is doing or what a great job they've got, or any of that stuff. What matters to me is: do they really have a heart and feel compassion for others? And I have to say that all my girlfriends have those qualities, which is why we will all go to the ends of the earth for each other. We phone, text or email each other all the time; and, last year, I started taking them away for an annual holiday. For this, I rented a villa in Spain and said: 'Come whenever you can', and we had the best time. Dr Kristy, my best friend from my schooldays, is still my best friend. Going through such dreadful bereavement experiences together when we were so young cemented us together for life. I love people who triumph over adversity, which is why *Forrest Gump* remains my favourite movie. Every time I watch it, and I must have seen it at least twenty times, I cry my eyes out. Kristy is also somebody who has triumphed over adversity, and I love her for that.

As far as my character is concerned, though, my fondest hope now is the same as it was in the beginning of my living this dream: that people will

269

always say of me: 'She hasn't changed.'

*   *   *

Today, as I sit here, preparing for the moment when I will put the final full stop to this, the last chapter of my book, my thoughts are constantly flitting to and from my dad, who is never far from my side.

Just before I went on holiday recently I went to see an amazing medium, Sally Morgan, who used to be Princess Diana's medium. The first message she gave me from my dad was that he would give anything right now to be part of what was happening for me. And so would I.

The next thing she said took my breath away, because there was no way she could have known that my dad used to whistle all the time.

'Your dad's whistling at me,' Sally said, 'and he wants you to know that whenever you hear whistling it means he's there; and that if you hear whistling outside your dressing-room, that's because he's guarding the door.'

I found that so comforting and moving because, as I've said before, I've never ceased to believe that he is still looking after me, still by my side, and I know if he could speak, he would smile and say something like: 'What now, love?'

'*Viva La Diva*, Dad. You'll be laughing at my tap dancing!'

But, just as I'm thinking about that I am returned to the present with a bump as my mobile rings and, in an instant, I am struck by the note of excitement in the disembodied voice.

'Katherine, guess what?' the voice says.

270

'What?' I reply, knowing in an instant that this is going to be one of those calls when, sooner or later, I will find myself exclaiming 'No way!'

And as the call comes to an end, I know that has been a call that is definitely going to set me on the road to the next momentous event in my life: but *what*, *where* and *when* will have to remain as a cliff-hanger for the present.

Right now, as my life has only stretched across twenty-seven years, I can only say, in those time-honoured words: 'To be continued . . .'

ACKNOWLEDGEMENTS

First and foremost, I would like to thank my mother Susan and sister Laura for all their love and support throughout the writing of this book.

For their patience and encouragement, my publisher Ian Marshall, Amanda Harris, Clare Wallis, Charlotte Cosic and all at Orion. To Neil Warnock, Marc Gerald and all at The Agency Group, London.

For their devotion and dedication to everything I do, Brian Lane, Tara Joseph and Juliane Thierne at Bandana Management.

To Lutz Bethge, Gerd Bostel, Atissa Tadjadod, Ingrid Roosen-Trinks, Kevin Boltman, Rhona Luthi, Sabine Graef and all at Montblanc for their continued support.

To the lovely Barbara Nash for helping me put all the pieces together. Thank you! I couldn't have done it without you!

For the special place they hold in my heart, the Taffia: Mum, Laura, Gavin, Louise, Cyril, Melanie, Jakob, Jason, Gavin, Kelly, Olivia, Jo, Alan, Naomi, Hannah, Ruth, Chris, Jeanne, Grifydd, Claire, Denzil, Lynsey. My friends: Kristy, Sophie, Katie, Jane, Kelly, Mary Rose, Edda, Edward, Ali, Vittorio, Oscar, Polloy, Jo and Dave, Chris, Steve, Fadi, Sharon, Cheryl, Sean and Darcey.

To my fans, who continue to support me in everything I do! You are the best! I hope you enjoy it!

Lastly, to everyone mentioned in the book— thank you for everything you have done for me. I am lucky to have you in my life!

Lots of love,
Katherine xxx